# Great Medical Discoveries

# Stem Cells

by Toney Allman

**LUCENT BOOKS**

*An imprint of Thomson Gale, a part of The Thomson Corporation*

**THOMSON**
—✳—
**GALE**

Detroit • New York • San Francisco • San Diego • New Haven, Conn. • Waterville, Maine • London • Munich

*For more information, contact*
Lucent Books
27500 Drake Rd.
Farmington Hills, MI 48331-3535
Or you can visit our Internet site at http://www.gale.com

LIBRARY OF CONGRESS CATALOGING-IN-PUBLICATION DATA

Allman, Toney.
  Stem cells / by Toney Allman.
    p. cm. — (Great medical discoveries)
  Includes bibliographical references and index.
  ISBN 1-59018-772-5 (hard cover : alk. paper)
  1. Stem cells—Juvenile literature. I. Title. II. Series.
QH588.S83A45 2005
616'.02774—dc22                                              2005012637

Printed in the United States of America

# CONTENTS

# FOREWORD

Throughout history, people have struggled to understand and conquer the diseases and physical ailments that plague us. Once in a while, a discovery has changed the course of medicine and sometimes, the course of history itself. The stories of these discoveries have many elements in common—accidental findings, sudden insights, human dedication, and most of all, powerful results. Many illnesses that in the past were essentially a death warrant for their sufferers are today curable or even virtually extinct. And exciting new directions in medicine promise a future in which the building blocks of human life itself—the genes—may be manipulated and altered to restore health or to prevent disease from occurring in the first place.

It has been said that an insight is simply a rearrangement of already-known facts, and as often as not, these great medical discoveries have resulted partly from a reexamination of earlier efforts in light of new knowledge. Nineteenth-century monk Gregor Mendel experimented with pea plants for years, quietly unlocking the mysteries of genetics. However, the importance of his findings went unnoticed until three separate scientists, studying cell division with a newly improved invention called a microscope, rediscovered his work decades after his death. French doctor Jean-Antoine Villemin's experiments with rabbits proved that tuberculosis was contagious, but his conclusions were politely ignored by the medical community until another doctor, Robert Koch of Germany, discovered the exact culprit—the tubercle bacillus germ—years later.

Accident, too, has played a part in some medical discoveries. Because the tuberculosis germ does not stain with dye as easily as other bacteria, Koch was able to see it only after he had let a treated slide sit far longer than he intended. An unwanted speck of mold led Englishman Alexander Fleming to recognize the bacteria-killing qualities of the penicillium fungi, ushering in the era of antibiotic "miracle drugs."

That researchers sometimes benefited from fortuitous accidents does not mean that they were bumbling amateurs who relied solely on luck. They were dedicated scientists whose work created the conditions under which such lucky events could occur; many sacrificed years of their lives to observation and experimentation. Sometimes the price they paid was higher. Rene Launnec, who invented the stethoscope to help him study the effects of tuberculosis, himself succumbed to the disease.

And humanity has benefited from these scientists' efforts. The formerly terrifying disease of smallpox has been eliminated from the face of the earth—the only case of the complete conquest of a once deadly disease. Tuberculosis, perhaps the oldest disease known to humans and certainly one of its most prolific killers, has been essentially wiped out in some parts of the world. Genetically engineered insulin is a godsend to countless diabetics who are allergic to the animal insulin that has traditionally been used to help them.

Despite such triumphs there are few unequivocal success stories in the history of great medical discoveries. New strains of tuberculosis are proving to be resistant to the antibiotics originally developed to treat them, raising the specter of a resurgence of the disease that has killed 2 billion people over the course of human history. But medical research continues on numerous fronts and will no doubt lead to still undreamed-of advancements in the future.

Each volume in the Great Medical Discoveries series tells the story of one great medical breakthrough—the first gropings for understanding, the pieces that came together and how, and the immediate and longer-term results. Part science and part social history, the series explains some of the key findings that have shaped modern medicine and relieved untold human suffering. Numerous primary and secondary source quotations enhance the text and bring to life all the drama of scientific discovery. Sidebars highlight personalities and convey personal stories. The series also discusses the future of each medical discovery—a future in which vaccines may guard against AIDS, gene therapy may eliminate cancer, and other as-yet unimagined treatments may become commonplace.

# INTRODUCTION

# The Promise of Stem Cell Research

When the state of California was considering a vote to fund stem cell research with tax dollars, a thirteen-year-old girl named Emma Klatman spoke publicly on behalf of this initiative: "I was diagnosed with Type 1 diabetes when I was seven years old. Suddenly, I was no longer a naïve young little girl, but a seven-year-old who had to test blood sugars with needles and give myself insulin shots for every morsel of food I ate. This is what I do every day and will have to for the rest of my life, if we do not find a cure. Vote for the cure!"[1]

The cure that Emma sought was once considered impossible, but stem cell research offers hope where there has never before been hope, not only for Emma but also for millions of people suffering previously untreatable diseases, disabilities, and injuries. Stem cells are the body's blanks, capable of generating and rebuilding all the cells in the body. On the embryonic level, they are the cells responsible for building a new, complete individual, the newborn baby. Science writer Ann B. Parson explains, "Stem cells are basic to the regeneration of every multicellular plant and animal, and as scientists discover more about them, these flexible worlds-unto-themselves should open our eyes to the presence of forces in Nature that are far greater than anything humans could imagine or invent."[2]

The "forces in Nature" that Parson describes are beginning to yield their secrets to scientists in laboratories around the world. As their research proceeds, these scientists believe that they will be able to manipulate and direct the stem cells they have discovered, using this ability to treat the untreatable and cure the uncurable. Emma Klatman is not the only one who views stem cell discoveries with excitement and optimism. Blindness, deafness, cancers, paralysis, birth defects, and inherited diseases may all be amenable to treatment with stem cell therapies. People with disabilities such as these have never been able to dream

*A researcher at a lab in Kansas City, Missouri, investigates stem cells, which may one day be used to cure diseases and heal injuries.*

of a future that includes sight, hearing, mobility, or health. Now they can.

With each new scientific announcement of experimental success, researchers raise the spirits of those with disabilities. Reports of scientific advances suggest that very soon society can expect a revolution in medicine. Stem cell therapies promise a breakthrough that may forever change how medicine is practiced. Yet not everybody supports stem cell research. For some people, its promise is clouded by profound moral and ethical concerns. These concerns arise primarily because embryonic stem cell research requires the destruction of human embryos.

Embryonic stem cells are just one type of stem cells, but they are of great interest to scientists because they have the flexibility to transform into all the many different parts and organs of a human body. Any disease or injury in any body part could potentially be treated with embryonic stem cells. Although everyone wants to see successful medical treatments for suffering people, many people strongly oppose cures that begin with the destruction of human embryos. They believe that a fertilized egg is already a human life, or at least sacred as potential human life, and therefore should be protected, not killed.

Although many scientists do not agree that early embryos are living beings, they recognize that their research can be disturbing and raises important ethical questions. As scientist Jane Maienschein says, "Human embryo research is, of course, first of all about science and about research. . . . Yet it is also about human embryos and making decisions about how to define what we will count as a life. . . . How, in particular, do we decide how to define when a life begins and what the appropriate boundaries and constraints on human embryo research should be?"[3]

The questions that Maienschein asks have been at the center of the controversy over stem cell research since human embryonic stem cells were first discovered in

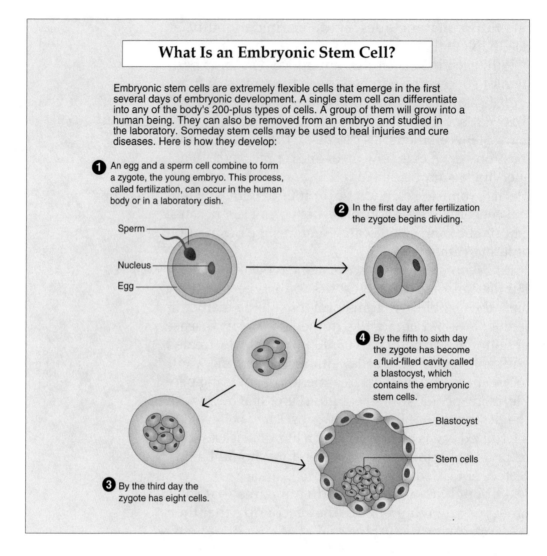

## What Is an Embryonic Stem Cell?

Embryonic stem cells are extremely flexible cells that emerge in the first several days of embryonic development. A single stem cell can differentiate into any of the body's 200-plus types of cells. A group of them will grow into a human being. They can also be removed from an embryo and studied in the laboratory. Someday stem cells may be used to heal injuries and cure diseases. Here is how they develop:

**1** An egg and a sperm cell combine to form a zygote, the young embryo. This process, called fertilization, can occur in the human body or in a laboratory dish.

**2** In the first day after fertilization the zygote begins dividing.

Sperm

Nucleus

Egg

**4** By the fifth to sixth day the zygote has become a fluid-filled cavity called a blastocyst, which contains the embryonic stem cells.

Blastocyst

Stem cells

**3** By the third day the zygote has eight cells.

1998. In the years that have followed, societies, governments, religions, and scientists have struggled to determine what course stem cell research should take. They have asked whether the protection of early embryonic life outweighs the value of research that could help millions of suffering people already born. Researchers hope that as society learns about the science of embryonic stem cells and as medical treatments using the cells become common, perceptions will change and embryonic cells will not be equated with developing babies. At this point, however, some people are not persuaded by scientific arguments that seem to redefine what an early embryo is and to deny that its cells are truly human life.

Despite the divided opinions about stem cell research, the research has not stopped. The controversy about embryonic stem cells has slowed progress in some areas, but the research goes on at universities and laboratories throughout the world. If one nation outlaws it, other countries allow and even encourage it, and the scientists continue their experimentation. The discoveries and the knowledge cannot be undone. The science goes forward.

Setting standards for scientific research is not easy, but the task is being addressed by governments and individuals around the world. Compromises are made; issues are clarified and argued; the needs and beliefs of different people are considered. Millions who await cures for their hopeless diseases do not care which kinds of stem cells are used. They just hope that the moral debate can be resolved and that the promise of stem cell research will reach fruition.

# CHAPTER 1

# The Discovery of Stem Cells

Dr. Ernest McCulloch was not trying to discover stem cells as he worked in his laboratory one Sunday afternoon in 1960. He was a medical researcher at the Ontario Cancer Institute in Toronto, Canada, who was studying cancer cells and how different cells in the body respond to radiation. Since he could not expose humans to radiation, he used laboratory mice in his experiments. First, he exposed the mice to such strong radiation that all their blood and bone marrow cells were killed. Then, he injected normal mouse bone marrow cells into some of the mice and irradiated bone marrow cells into others. Bone marrow is where new blood cells are grown, both in mice and in people. Since radiation is often used to kill cancer, McCulloch wanted to know how sensitive bone marrow cells are to radiation.

## Puzzling Bumps

That Sunday, McCulloch was examining the tissues from several of the mice, looking for differences in their blood or bone marrow. He could find no differences at all between mice with irradiated bone marrow and mice with normal bone marrow. The experiment might have been a failure, but McCulloch noticed something strange under his microscope. In all the mice's spleens were some odd-looking, small whitish bumps. Mouse

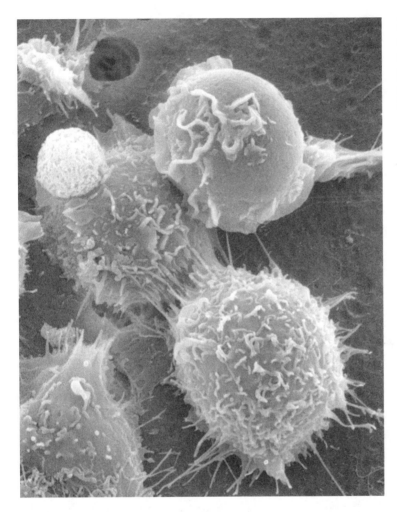

*Bone marrow stem cells, shown extremely magnified in this photo, give rise to every type of blood cell.*

spleens, along with their bone marrow, grow new blood cells. As he stared at the bumps, McCulloch realized that the number of bumps in each spleen equaled the number of injections he had given each mouse.

The next morning, McCulloch got to work early. As his partner, James Till, walked down the hall, McCulloch ran out to meet him. "Look at this!" he called. McCulloch had plotted on a graph the number of cell injections and the number of spleen bumps. They matched up perfectly. Together, the two scientists got to work and discovered that each little bump was a colony of cells. They named the bumps "spleen

colonies"[4] and surmised that the colonies were created by a single cell. They did not know what that cell
was or where it was, but they wrote a scientific paper
describing their findings and suggesting that bone marrow cells grew from this single cell.

## The Birth of Stem Cell Science

For a couple of years, no other scientists paid much
attention to the paper by Till and McCulloch, but the
two scientists and their students kept researching their
discovery. In 1963, they were able to publish new
research proving that the colonies were formed from
single cells that were able to duplicate themselves and
create colonies of different kinds of blood cells. Blood
cells seemed to *stem* from these cells.

McCulloch and Till had discovered adult stem cells,
so called because they exist in the body after birth.
Blood-forming adult stem cells were the first stem cells
to be discovered, but other scientists found stem cells
responsible for the growth and replacement of cells
in other organs as well. Stem cell science was born, and
excited scientists around the world set out to learn the
amazing properties of stem cells, the cells from which
all other cells arise.

## What Are Cells?

All living things, including humans, are made up of
cells. They are the building blocks of life. Each cell is
a microscopic body surrounded by a membrane, somewhat like a soap bubble. Within the cell is the nucleus.
Inside the nucleus are the chemical bases, the DNA,
that make up the thousands of genes that are arranged
along the twenty-three pairs of chromosomes in the
human body. The DNA writes a code, like the letters
that form the words in a giant book, that determines
how each human body develops and functions. The
genetic information within each cell has been there
since the individual was a single cell—a fertilized egg—
that divided and divided until it became a mass of

# The Stuff of Life

A cell is a tiny marvel of chemical activity. Within its protective membrane, all its chemical signals and genetic material are protected from outside interference, except for the nutrition and oxygen that cross into the cell through its pores. Inside the balloon of the membrane is a jellylike substance called cytoplasm. It holds the cell's small organs, called organelles. The endoplasmic reticulum is an organelle that is the roadway system in the cytoplasm that carries the cell materials where they need to be taken. Ribosomes are stuck on the sides of the roads. They build the proteins for the cell and send them off along the cell's highway system. Lysosomes break up and digest food for energy. Mitochondria also digest food and act as the cell's power generators. Other organelles act as storage tanks or strengthen and build up proteins to keep the cell healthy.

The nucleus, in the center of the cell, is its brain and directs all the cell activities. The cell's highway system carries chemical messages to and from the nucleus. In humans, the nucleus contains twenty-three pairs of rodlike structures called chromosomes. Arranged along the chromosomes are about thirty-five thousand genes. Genes carry information that tells cells to make certain proteins. Each protein will perform a special function. Proteins do the work in the body. Most of the DNA in any particular cell is inactive. Only the instructions that are needed to direct that cell's activity operate.

Body cells are microscopic and come in many different shapes and sizes, depending on their functions. No matter what their size, shape, or function, all cells are efficient factories that are essential for healthy life. When things go wrong in a cell or it dies, stem cells must wake up and regenerate these complicated little factories.

**Anatomy of a Cell**

Cell membrane

Chromosome

Ribosome

Mitochondria

Nucleus

Lysosome

Cytoplasm

Endoplasmic reticulum

developing cells, called an embryo. Directed by the DNA, the multiplying embryonic cells organize themselves until they are stacked and grouped into the tissues and organs of a developing baby, called a fetus.

By the time the baby is born, it is made of billions of cells that have specialized into heart cells, bone cells, skin cells, brain cells, and all the more than two hundred other kinds of cells that make up a human body. Each cell has its specific job to do. Heart cells beat. Cells in the pancreas produce insulin. Eye cells send light signals to the brain. Directed by the chemical messages of DNA, the cells perform the necessary functions that maintain life. When they become old or damaged, the cells must be replaced or else the individual will become sickened or disabled. New cells must grow if the body is to remain healthy. This is the job of the adult stem cells.

## New Cells for Old: The Stem Cells' Job

Stem cells are special cells with unique abilities. Most important, stem cells are unspecialized. They do not beat like heart cells, for example, or carry oxygen in the bloodstream. Yet, given the right chemical signals, stem cells can divide, replicate themselves, and then differentiate into specific body cells. Skin stem cells, for instance, differentiate into new skin cells. All stem cells are also capable of proliferation. This means that they will sometimes divide over and over, making new stem cells by the millions, without differentiating into specialized cells. Because they are unspecialized and able to proliferate and differentiate, stem cells are the very stuff of life.

By the time the baby has become a child or an adult, he or she has trillions of cells. Billions of blood cells, for instance, make up human blood. The red blood cells are different from other body cells. They no longer have nuclei with DNA, but they still carry oxygen and fuel to the organs in the body. However, red blood cells live only about four months and must be replaced regularly. In the bone marrow, in the center of the bones of human beings, are stem cells called hematopoietic stem cells,

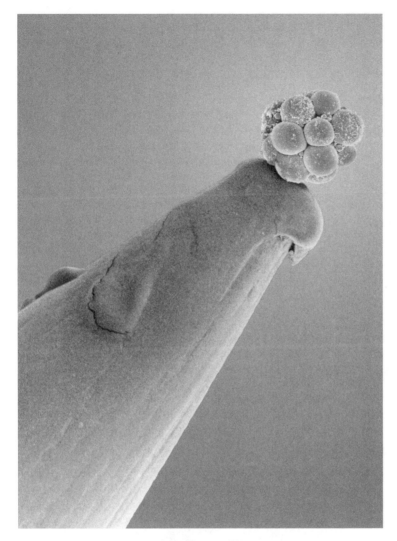

*This three-day-old embryo, photographed on the point of a pin, is the tiny package that has the capacity to develop into a complete human being.*

which generate the new blood cells. Skin cells and other cells that are often damaged or scraped off must be continually replaced or regenerated by stem cells as well.

Scientists knew that some mechanism existed within the body's chemical code that directed the replacement of body cells. However, until the landmark work of Ernest McCulloch and James Till, no one knew what this mechanism was. The discovery of adult stem cells told scientists how cells were renewed. With this knowledge, researchers could hope to learn to correct diseases and injuries in which cells were damaged but stem cells failed to replace them. Skin that was badly burned might be regenerated by skin stem cells that could grow new skin. Blood diseases such as leukemia might be treated with hematopoietic stem cells. But first, scientists would have to figure out how to isolate these stem cells, grow them in laboratory dishes, and "turn them on" so that they would regenerate new tissues and blood.

## Isolating the First Adult Stem Cells

Irving Weissman was a medical student at Stanford University in California when he read the papers that Till and McCulloch published. He remembered later, "It was like a light bulb went on. It had a massive impact. Everyone's work on hematopoiesis (the development of blood cells) and stem cells is based on them."[5] The papers had a great influence on Weissman. After graduating from medical school, he devoted his professional life to stem cell research. It was one thing to know that stem cells existed; it was quite another to find them in bone marrow and isolate them in the laboratory. Only about one in every ten or fifteen thousand cells in bone marrow is a stem cell, and this valuable cell looks no different from any of the others. Weissman was determined to find those elusive cells.

After decades of patient work, Weissman finally isolated stem cells from the blood of laboratory mice through a detailed process of elimination. In 1988, he injected these few cells into mice whose own blood cells had been destroyed by radiation. The laboratory cells created a whole system of healthy blood in the mouse bone marrow, proving that they were adult stem cells. Weissman was thrilled. "It was really unbelievable," he said. "We had been working in systems where you'd have to transfer several hundred thousand to a million bone marrow cells to save a lethally irradiated mouse. So now we could do it with 30 to 100 cells. That meant we could hope to do the same in humans."[6]

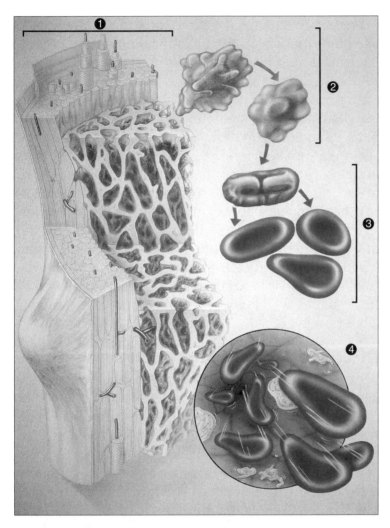

*Stem Cells in Bone Marrow: (1) Cutaway view of a bone showing the marrow inside, (2) adult stem cells produced in bone marrow, (3) stem cells becoming red blood cells, and (4) red blood cells circulating in blood with other types of cells.*

## Human Adult Stem Cells

Weissman's next effort was to find stem cells in human bone marrow. He and his colleagues could not irradiate a human being, so they figured out a way to put human bone marrow cells into mice. Then they used radiation, injection, and the process of elimination to separate human stem cells from the human bone marrow in these special mice. In April 1992, Weissman's team was able to report to the world that they had found the human hematopoietic (blood-forming) stem cell.

Weissman's success inspired immediate attempts to use hematopoietic stem cells for medical treatment. Almost all cancers require heavy doses of radiation and chemotherapy to kill the cancer cells, but these powerful poisons also kill healthy blood cells. Cancer specialists tried injecting hematopoietic stem cells into patients subjected to radiation and chemotherapy. The effort was not always successful, but it saved the lives of many more cancer patients than in the past. Stem cells seemed to promise a revolution in medicine if scientists could learn how to give them the chemical message to turn on or make them differentiate into the desired kind of cell. Scientists around the world began searching for stem cells in other body organs and tissues. If healthy blood could be created in place of poisoned blood, who knew what other kinds of treatments were possible?

## Discovering Brain Stem Cells

Because brains rarely regenerate or heal when they are damaged, scientists thought they probably had no stem cells, but in 1992, brain stem cells were also discovered. Again, the discovery was a fortuitous accident. Dr. Samuel Weiss and his scientific team at the University of Calgary in Canada were growing neurons, or nerve cells, in a nutritious bath of chemicals in a petri dish. They hoped to show that the chemical bath could keep fetal mouse nerve cells alive so they could be studied. The experiment failed, but one student forgot his petri dish and left it in the lab's incubator for a couple of weeks. When he finally remembered the culture and looked at it, he found some strange globes of cells floating in the bath. They were not neurons being kept alive; further experiments proved that they were stem cells. The lab team theorized that if neural stem cells existed in fetal mouse brains, they must exist in adult mouse brains, too. Weiss remembered, "I thought it was a truly unlikely phenomenon. But we thought 'If they did exist wouldn't that set the world on its ear?' We took adult mouse brains and we got the same growth of neural stem cells."[7] In 2000, Irving Weissman, at Stanford University, proved that the same neural cells existed in human brains and could be isolated in the laboratory. These stem cells sat silently in the brain, even when it was damaged, but in laboratory dishes they could be encouraged to divide and grow.

## Skin Emergency!

Scientists have discovered that skin has more stem cells than any other body organ or tissue. They believe that skin needs the most stem cells because it is so often damaged. If a person is slicing an apple, for example, lets the knife slip, and cuts a finger, the damaged cells send emergency signals to the stem cells in the skin. The stem cells have been in a resting state, and the chemical signals from the injured cells activate them. Activation takes about twenty-four hours to complete, but once completely awakened the stem cells begin to divide. Each stem cell divides into two daughter cells. One daughter cell differentiates into a skin cell and moves to the area of the wound. The other daughter cell remains undifferentiated so that it can make more stem cells. Skin stem cells keep dividing like this until the injured area is repopulated with healthy skin cells. Because only half the dividing stem cells differentiate, the skin never loses its population of stem cells. They return to a resting state, ready for the next time they are needed.

*Through the process of mitosis, a skin cell divides into two new cells.*

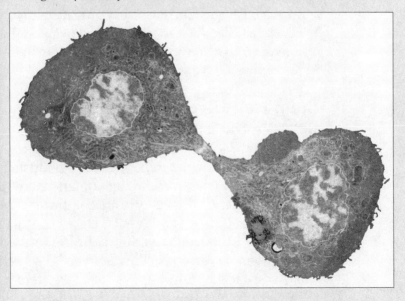

## Stem Cells in Eyes

Inspired by Weiss's success, Derek van der Kooy at the University of Toronto in Canada searched for and found adult stem cells in the retina of the eye in 2000. "The eye is a place where you'd never think of looking for stem cells because when the eye is damaged, no new cells would be created. When you're blind, you're blind. There's nothing you can do about that,"[8] van der Kooy said. But, he thought, stem cells might be in the eye, since it is directly connected to the brain. Van der Kooy found about one hundred stem cells in the retinas of mice. Later, he discovered that human retinas contain about ten thousand stem cells. No one knows why such stem cells sit quietly in the eye and are not directed by their DNA to turn on to repair injuries, but van der Kooy was tremendously excited to find them. Suddenly, he realized that blindness might be curable if these stem cells could be grown into new eye cells in the lab. He speculated,

> It might be incredibly useful therapeutically. Because here is an easy population of cells you can get out (from eye donors), they're easy to maintain and grow in culture and when you differentiate them, they produce the major type of cell that's missing in a lot of blind people—the photoreceptors. We can produce huge numbers of those photoreceptors for the human eye.[9]

## Stem Cells Everywhere

By 2005, medical researchers were no longer struggling with how to isolate or grow adult stem cells in the laboratory. Building on the successes of scientists over the preceding few years, researchers determined that stem cells can be found throughout the human body. In Australia, at Griffith University, Dr. Alan Mackay-Sim discovered stem cells inside the lining of the human nose. Given the progress that stem cell researchers are making, MacKay-Sim hopes that these stem cells can be grown in test tubes and differentiated into brain cells, heart cells, and more. He explains, "We have got an adult stem cell which is accessible to everybody and we can grow lots of these cells and turn them into many other cell types."[10]

Also in 2005, scientists in the United States isolated heart stem cells in mice. In a test tube, these stem cells grew into heart cells that beat in time with each other, just as normal cells do within mouse hearts. To the surprise of many scientists, stem cells apparently can be found everywhere in adult bodies, whether animals or people. The scientists who have been researching stem cells believe that their discoveries will soon be used to correct diseases and injuries that are without cures today.

Freda Miller, who isolated human skin stem cells in 2001, says, "I'm very optimistic. I don't know which disease it will be. I don't know if it will be stroke or Parkinson's or spinal cord injury. But I think we will be able to help a population that can't be helped now. I wouldn't be doing this work if I wasn't a believer."[11] The discoverers of stem cells are all believers in the medical possibilities of the cells they have found. However, another amazing kind of stem cell has been discovered, and it may hold even more promise than the adult stem cells that fill scientists with such hope.

# CHAPTER 2

# The Discovery of Embryonic Stem Cells

At the same time people like Irving Weissman were researching adult stem cells, other scientists were searching for the secrets of the fertilized egg. A fertilized egg is really a super stem cell. It is a single cell that gives rise to a complete individual, yet it is barely visible to the sharpest naked eye. When this super stem cell is turned on, a new life begins. As the fertilized egg divides and develops, embryonic stem cells appear and create all the cells that make up a living body. If scientists could discover and isolate these stem cells, they might be able to control the way cells grow and perhaps to conquer inherited diseases, cancers, and devastating injuries.

## Secrets of the Egg

As a human fertilized egg, or zygote, grows, it goes through several identifiable stages. First, in a process called mitosis, the zygote splits in two, making identical cells, each of which has all the chromosomes and DNA of the original cell. These cells divide into four cells and then eight. Up to this point, each cell retains its super stem-ness and therefore is totipotent. Each cell is capable of giving rise to every cell needed to grow an embryo, a fetus, and then a person. By the time

# Development of the Embryo

When a sperm penetrates an egg and fertilizes it, the egg has just been released from the ovary and is entering the fallopian tube. The fertilized egg, or zygote, slowly falls through the tube on its journey to the womb. During its first cell divisions, it is still floating. When this zygote arrives in the womb, it has become a blastocyst with its pluripotent stem cells. The chemicals in the uterus signal to the blastocyst that it is in the correct environment. If all goes well, the outer shell of the blastocyst sends out little fingers of cells that burrow into the wall of the womb and implant there. Not until the blastocyst has implanted do any cells begin to differentiate into cells of an organism, so many scientists do not consider it a true embryo. Instead, they call it a preimplantation embryo. Research has revealed that as many as three-fourths of all preimplantation embryos fail, do not implant, and simply die without anyone ever having been aware that they existed. Many scientists, therefore, do not consider that a life has begun until the pre-embryo implants and becomes an embryo.

*A human embryo typically implants itself into the uterine wall eight days after fertilization.*

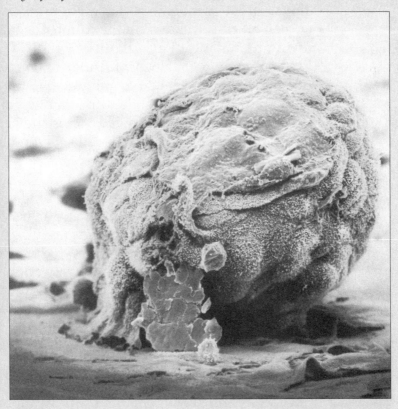

there are sixteen cells, totipotency is gone. The cells are already beginning to differentiate slightly.

By the fourth day of growth, the embryo has become a ball of cells called a blastocyst. The cells of the outer layer of the ball will become the placenta, which carries nourishment from the mother to the developing embryo. The inner cells of the blastocyst are pluripotent stem cells, which will become a fetus and then a baby. Unlike totipotent stem cells, pluripotent stem cells cannot form all the cells necessary to create a new life, such as those that give rise to the placenta. Pluripotent stem cells, however, can become any cell in the body.

By day five or six, the blastocyst has floated down the fallopian tube and into the uterus, or womb. It looks like a fluid-filled balloon, about 120 cells large and about half the size of the period at the end of this sentence. If all goes well within the womb, the blastocyst now implants into the wall of the womb. Then, the dividing cells will organize into different layers, clump together, begin specializing, and develop the tissues and organs of a fetus. By the time eight weeks have passed, the embryo is considered a fetus and has developed multipotent adult stem cells. The embryonic pluripotent stem cells are no more.

## Inspiration from a Strange Source

Because pluripotent stem cells from the blastocyst can become any kind of body cell, they are the cells that hold the most promise for understanding how life begins and what goes wrong that causes disease, but isolating these stem cells in the laboratory was very hard. Scientists were sure embryonic stem cells existed, but their efforts to discover them yielded only frustration for many years.

During the 1970s, Martin Evans and Gail Martin were working together in England, trying to control cancer cells and keep them alive. Many cancer tumor cells are very similar to stem cells in the way that they divide and divide with no apparent control. As the two scientists carefully isolated stem-like cells of tumors and grew them in petri dishes, they made an amazing discovery. In the chemical baths of petri dishes, proliferating tumor cells could clump together into little round balls and start to specialize—into heart cells, muscle cells, and more! Martin said, "It suddenly clicked. [They] were mimicking normal development."[12] Realizing that cancer cells were like stem cells gone wrong inspired both scientists to search for embryonic stem cells and learn how normal development proceeded. Later, Evans and Martin moved to separate labs of their own, and both began to search for a way to isolate and grow embryonic stem cells.

## Mouse Embryonic Stem Cells

Gail Martin moved to the University of California in San Francisco, where she carefully removed three-day-old embryos from pregnant laboratory mice. She dissected the embryos under a microscope and pulled out the inner cells. The embryos were so tiny that, as careful as she was, she often failed to retrieve whole, single cells. Even when she succeeded, the cells often died in her petri dish. Stem cells were not identifiable by how they looked. The only way to know that the cells were stem cells was to see if they divided and grew, and for years they did not.

Finally, Martin developed a nutritious chemical bath that used tumor cells, which grow easily, to jump-start her embryo cells' growth. In 1981, this technique succeeded, and she had stem cells that stayed alive and grew in the petri dishes. In a paper describing her success, she dubbed these stem cells "embryonic stem cells," or ES cells for short.

## Simultaneous Success

At the same time that Gail Martin made her discovery, Martin Evans, at Cambridge University in England, discovered and isolated stem cells from embryos, too.

*In 1998 James Thomson of the University of Wisconsin–Madison successfully grew human embryonic stem cells in the laboratory.*

He used a different laboratory method than Martin. He also had faced the difficulty of the tininess of the mouse embryo and the impossibility of extracting the few stem cells from the blastocyst. He solved the problem by figuring out a way to keep the tiny embryo floating in the mother mouse's uterus, instead of implanting. This made the embryo grow bigger and make more stem cells, without developing or differentiating in any way. Then he extracted the embryo, pulled it apart to get the stem cells, and placed them in a nutritional bath in a petri dish. After a few days, the cells began to divide and grow. Martin was thrilled. He was actually growing embryonic stem cells from an animal, and he was able to prevent them from differentiating. He said, "In a normal embryo there's an inevitable time progression going on, but taking them out into tissue culture, into the petri dish, they're marking time. And we can keep these cells, still with their ability to develop in any way, as millions and millions of cells, in our petri dish."[13]

## From Mouse Embryos to Human Embryos

Once mouse embryonic stem cells had been discovered, scientists were determined to find human embryonic stem cells as well. James Thomson, at the University of Wisconsin–Madison, was one of those scientists. By the 1990s, he had already found ES cells in monkeys, so he knew he could do the same in humans. He believed that the discovery of human ES cells had unlimited potential to help scientists find cures for human diseases. Yet he was worried about the ethics of such research.

In 1995, the U.S. Congress had outlawed federal funding for any human embryo research because such research meant destroying an embryo. To many people, that was equivalent to destroying a human life. Thomson did not think a blastocyst was the same as a baby or even a fetus, but he sought out friends and colleagues and asked their opinions. Said his friend, Norman Fost, a professor of pediatrics, "Jamie cared deeply about doing the right thing. He appreciated the larger social context and understood that others might be upset about what he was doing."[14] Thomson also talked to the research review board at the university, which discussed and approved his request to search for human embryonic stem cells. A private company offered to fund Thomson's search since he could not ask for research money from the federal government.

## Isolating Human ES Cells

Having decided that searching for cells that could eliminate human suffering was a moral thing to do, Thomson planned to collect the embryos for his search from an in vitro fertilization clinic at the University of Wisconsin. In vitro clinics fertilize eggs in petri dishes for couples who have difficulty getting pregnant. The egg is taken from the woman, fertilized with sperm taken from the man, grown to the early embryo stage in a petri dish, and then implanted in the woman's womb. If all goes well, a healthy baby is born. Such pregnancies often fail, however, so the clinics retrieve and fertilize many eggs from the woman at the same time. The extra embryos are saved and frozen so that the couple can try again if the first implantation fails. If it succeeds, and the couple does

*A scientist inspects embryos for use in in vitro fertilization. Thomson conducted his research using embryos from an in vitro fertilization clinic.*

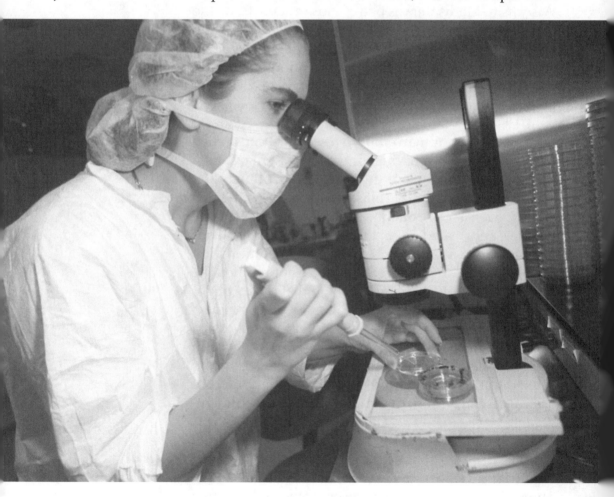

not want more children, the leftover embryos are not wanted and are usually discarded. These unwanted, leftover embryos were the ones that Thomson wanted to use for his research. First he got the permission of the couples who were willing to donate these embryos. Then he went to work.

In a small room at the in vitro clinic, Thomson and his team unfroze the embryos, grew them to the blastocyst stage, and then carefully separated out the stem cells from the inner mass. They placed the cells in dishes enriched with chemicals to nourish the cells. Then they allowed the cells to divide while they carefully watched the cultures to make sure that the cells did not differentiate. Very often, the team had to separate the dividing cells into extra dishes to keep them from clumping together and starting to specialize. Weeks went by, and the dishes of human embryonic stem cells kept dividing and proliferating. When stem cells divide and proliferate this long, scientists call them immortal. Thomson had succeeded, and his stem cells remained immortal, as long as he kept them separated. Once, however, a dish was not watched carefully enough, and the stem cells began to differentiate. Thomson's team looked on in amazement as the ES cells specialized into heart cells and began to beat together. One member of the team remembered, "People in the lab were in awe. It was so symbolic of the therapies these cells stood for."[15] In 1998, Thomson announced to the world that he had discovered human embryonic stem cells.

## Another ES Cell Success

At the same time, John Gearhart at Johns Hopkins University in Maryland also announced he had successfully isolated and grown human embryonic stem cells. Gearhart had grown his ES cells from fetuses that had been aborted at a nearby abortion clinic. Like Thomson, Gearhart had worried about the ethics of his

## The Bad Seeds

Teratomas are rare cancerous tumors that usually grow in the testes of males or the ovaries of females. For hundreds of years they were considered works of the devil, but today scientists know that they are caused by stem cells gone wrong. Testes and ovaries are the organs that produce sperm and eggs. The stem cells that cause teratomas are like mirror images of the embryonic stem cells that give rise to new individuals. Mistakes in the DNA that tell stem cells when to turn on and off again cause the cancer stem cells to divide wildly and give rise to tumors. These tumors, however, are not like ordinary tumors. As their cells proliferate, some also differentiate and crazily give rise to body tissues that belong elsewhere. Teratomas have been found with hunks of hair, small teeth, pieces of skin, beating heart cells, and bumps of bone—all mixed into a terrible stew of cancer.

It was teratoma cells from mice that Gail Martin and Martin Evans watched differentiate in petri dishes in the laboratory. As the cancer cells gave rise to normal body cells, the researchers felt sure that these cells had counterparts—real embryonic stem cells—that behaved correctly and gave rise to all the cells in the body. One type of stem cell was normal, the other malignant. Only the differences in their genetic codes distinguished them. The knowledge that Martin and Evans gained about the nutrition necessary to grow embryonic stem cells came from their experience with growing teratoma cells. In a way, a strange cancerous tumor led to the discovery of embryonic stem cells.

*The large, irregular shape of this ovarian cell reveals that it is cancerous.*

research. He read all the books he could find about abortion. He studied laws and policies from many different countries. He thought hard about his own beliefs. Finally, he decided that he was at peace with the issue. He said, "My shelves are now laden with books and articles, but even after extensive reading and continual discussions, I remain convinced of my position." Gearhart concluded that it would be wrong to waste fetal tissue that was about to be thrown away. He explained, "The potential for these unique, versatile cells for human biologic studies and medicine is enormous. These cells will rapidly let us study human processes in a way we couldn't before. Instead of having to rely on mice or other substitutes for human tissues, we'll have a unique resource that we can start applying to medicine."[16]

Gearhart's team grew human ES cells that divided and proliferated. The scientists were even able to prove that the cells were pluripotent by showing that the cell cultures retained the ability to differentiate into any kind of body cell. With this success, Gearhart foresaw the ability not only to grow but also to manipulate and direct human ES cells and then medically inject them into people whose own cells were damaged. He said, "We have demonstrations that we can form virtually any cell type that is present in the body. We can grow these cells in very large numbers, and furthermore we have shown in animal models that these cells can be transplanted and they can function. They can assume the functions of the cells that are desired."[17]

## But Is It Right?

Gearhart, Thomson, and many other scientists were tremendously excited by their newfound knowledge, but when their discoveries were reported to the general public, a firestorm of controversy resulted. Many people, especially religious groups, were horrified. They believed that scientists were making and destroying potential human beings in laboratory petri dishes. Pope John Paul II, for instance, declared that human life is sacred from the moment an egg is fertilized. Under his direction, the Catholic Church announced that the destruction, or what it called "ablation," of embryos to grow human ES cells is wrong. The church statement read, in part, "The ablation of the inner cell mass (ICM) of the blastocyst, which critically and irremediably damages the human embryo, curtailing its development, is a *gravely immoral* act and consequently is *gravely illicit*."[18] Many other religious groups equated human ES cell research with abortion and killing babies.

Other people worried about the potential to abuse human ES cell research. They could imagine a time in the future when scientists would be able to grow embryos far past the blastocyst stage in the lab, and then destroy the fetus to harvest its organs or tissues for medical use. People also knew that the capability to

*Wearing protective clothing to prevent contamination, a biologist at the UK stem cell bank in London, the first of its kind in the world, prepares embryos for storage.*

alter genes in embryos would soon become a reality. Then scientists would have the ability to make "designer" babies with whatever genetic characteristics they wished.

Gearhart worried about this possibility, too. After he succeeded with his laboratory ES cells, he had his whole team read Aldous Huxley's 1932 science fiction book, *Brave New World*. The book describes a world in which scientists grow embryos into babies who are copies, or clones, of each other. Through the manipulation of their genes they are designed to function as slaves. It is a frightening vision of the future. Gearhart said, "If we are successful in genetically manipulating our cells, it will mean that now, for the first time, we are instructing our cells to behave as we wish. What enormous powers will we then possess? How will we use them? Who will decide?"[19] If scientists developed the ability to conquer disease with stem cells, they would also face serious questions about the ethics and morality of their work.

## Defending the Research

People with untreatable diseases and injuries, however, as well as their families and doctors, were not worrying about science fiction futures. They were strongly supportive of human ES cell research. For the first time, they had reason to hope for cures. Scientists such as Gearhart and Thomson were determined to continue their research and bring medical treatments to these people. As one scientist said about human ES cell therapies, "We are ethically and morally obliged to pursue them for the benefit of those who suffer."[20]

Even though he worked only with adult stem cells, Irving Weissman also tried to answer some of the critics of human ES cell research. He remarked,

> You can't say the word embryo without people thinking of a fetus that has arms, legs, a head and so on. (Embryos

at the preimplantation blastocyst stage have no recognizable body parts or organs, only about 60 cells in the inner cell mass, and these have no resemblance to any cell in an adult tissue or organ.) . . . There's no kidneys, there's no hearts; I mean there's no nothing.[21]

Still, the arguments over destroying human embryos did not go away. The isolation and growth of human ES cells is still controversial, but some sources of stem cells are supported by everyone. These stem cells are already saving lives.

# CHAPTER 3

# The In-Between Stem Cells

In 1999, Nathan Salley, a fourteen-year-old American boy, underwent a dangerous experiment in order to save his life. Doctors killed all the blood cells in his body and injected him with stem cells from the umbilical cord of a newborn baby in Spain. The umbilical cord connects a fetus to its placenta, the life-support system for the developing baby. The placenta is attached to the mother's womb, and it is here that her blood transfers nutrition and oxygen to the fetus through its umbilical cord. When a baby is born, doctors cut the umbilical cord and usually throw it away along with the placenta. Inside the umbilical cord, however, are about 3 ounces (88.7ml.) of blood that contains stem cells. These cord blood stem cells saved Nathan's life. When Nathan was sixteen years old, in 2001, he told the story of his long journey to this life-saving treatment.

## Saving Nathan

Nathan was eleven years old when he was diagnosed with leukemia, a cancer of the blood. "It was a terrible time, but I always tried to look on the bright side. . . . Friends were very supportive, but the cancer treatment was awful. Cranial radiation exhausted me and chemotherapy caused me terrible nausea," he remembered. "For eighteen months, I had chemotherapy, for

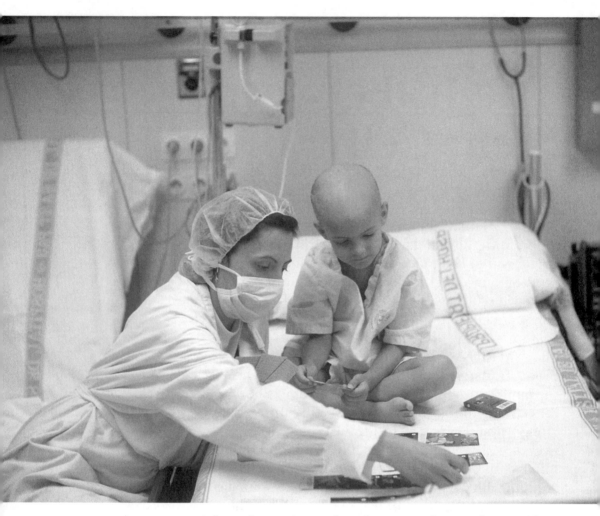

*A young leukemia patient, who has lost his hair as a result of chemotherapy, plays cards with his mother in his hospital bed.*

eighty-six to ninety-four hours each month. . . . I lost my hair and appetite, but I tried hard to do as many things as I could—for life to be as normal as possible."[22] Chemotherapy and radiation are powerful poisons that kill body cells, such as hair cells, bone marrow cells, and blood cells, as well as cancer cells. Doctors must perform a careful balancing act between using enough medicine to kill the cancer but not so much that the patient is killed. In Nathan's case, his doctors were successful at first, and Nathan finally thought that the treatments were over and that his cancer was gone. When he was fourteen, however, the leukemia returned. His body could not tolerate being poisoned with treatments anymore. Doctors predicted that he would die within five years unless they could kill all his blood cells along with the cancer cells and replace his blood with new blood.

## Cord Blood and Transplants

Nathan's family wanted to help by donating bone marrow to produce blood for him for transplantation, but

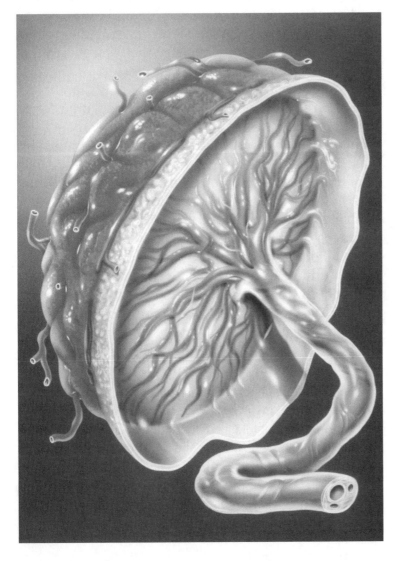

*The placenta and the umbilical cord supply the fetus with nutrients and oxygen from its mother's blood supply.*

they could not. All human blood cells carry genetic factors or proteins called antigens that are specific to each individual. Six different antigens exist, and different people have different antigens on their cells. If these antigens do not match, donor blood can make patients very, very sick or even kill them. Many people match with one or two of the antigens, but a donor match is best when all six antigens are the same. If they are not, the patient's immune system attacks and rejects the blood donation as if it were a foreign disease that must be destroyed. No one in Nathan's family was a good match for him, but Nathan's doctors did not give up. Through an international registry, they discovered that cord blood from a baby in Spain was available that matched Nathan's blood six for six.

Nathan said, "Cord blood transplants were becoming more widely used by 1999, but were still experimental. Physicians assured us a cord blood transplant was my best chance for life and would reduce the likelihood of rejecting the transplant. After prayerful consideration, my parents and I followed their advice."[23] Nathan at fourteen needed much more blood than the 3 ounces (88.7 ml.) in a tiny newborn baby's cord blood. Doctors decided to give Nathan some of the blood and use the rest to grow cord blood stem cells in the laboratory. Because stem cells can proliferate, the doctors hoped to grow enough blood stem cells for Nathan's needs.

Doctors were ready to try the transplant in the summer of 1999. Nathan described what happened next:

> Before the transplant could take place my doctors had to completely kill my own leukemia-producing blood cells with three days of total body radiation, followed by more intense chemotherapy. Then, the transplant took place in two phases. I received about 60 percent of the donated cord blood cells on June 29, 1999, when they arrived from Spain. The remaining cells were sent to the lab to be expanded. I was transfused with these cells ten days later on July 9, 1999.

It was an agonizing wait for my blood counts to begin to recover. I could not eat for two to three weeks. Thankfully, I am in complete remission today. Regular testing continues to show no leukemia present in my body. The transplanted cells have built a brand new bone marrow system for me.[24]

## Cord Blood Stem Cells

The cord blood stem cells that saved Nathan's life were adult stem cells, but since they were from the umbilical cord, they were younger and more immature than other adult stem cells. This immaturity was a great advantage for Nathan's treatment. Even

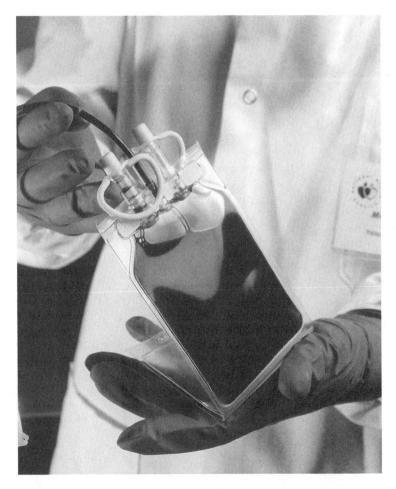

This umbilical cord blood, in storage at the London Cord Blood Bank, could potentially be used to help fight such diseases as leukemia.

# Jelly Cells

In 2005, scientists at the University of Toronto in Canada discovered a new source of stem cells in the umbilical cord. These stem cells are not in the cord blood, nor are they hematopoietic stem cells. They are in the Wharton's jelly, a jellylike tissue surrounding the blood vessels in the umbilical cord. These stem cells are mesenchymal cells, which are bone- and cartilage-forming cells. Mesenchymal cells appear in cord blood, too, but they are rare. Only one cell in every 200 million cord blood cells is a mesenchymal cell. In the Wharton's jelly, one in 300 cells is a stem cell. The Toronto researchers were very excited to find this stem cell source because these cells could be used for growing new bone for bone diseases. The scientists extracted these cells from the Wharton's jelly and grew them in petri dishes. Their next step will be to experiment with them in animals in order to develop successful treatments. Today, the Wharton's jelly from umbilical cords is thrown away when cord blood is collected and banked. The Toronto discovery, however, may change that soon.

*A jellylike tissue called Wharton's jelly surrounds the umbilical vein, shown highly magnified in this photo.*

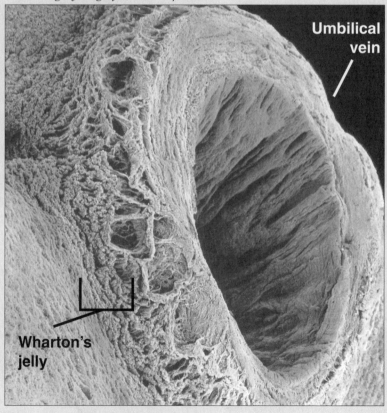

Umbilical
vein

Wharton's
jelly

with a six for six antigen match, patients' bodies often reject donor blood, for reasons that are unclear to doctors. Cord blood cells, because they are not fully mature, are more easily accepted than other adult stem cells from unrelated donors. Nathan's body did not reject the donation of these immature stem cells. Also, the stem cells proliferated easily in the laboratory. Without this proliferation, Nathan would not have received enough cells to save him before he died. Cord blood cells do not have the pluripotency of embryonic stem cells. They cannot become any kind of cell in the body, but they were able to differentiate into the kinds of blood cells that Nathan needed.

Nathan was one of the early patients who proved that a tiny amount of cord blood was just as good for treating leukemia as perfectly matched hematopoietic adult stem cells would be. Because perfect matches for people who need hematopoietic stem cell transplants are hard to find, scientists were excited to learn that cord blood cells were a good substitute. Since the time of Nathan's experimental cure, much more has been learned about the value of cord blood stem cells, and much more cord blood is available for medical treatment.

## Cord Blood Banks

In 2003, the U.S. Congress established the National Cord Blood Stem Cell Bank Network to fund and support the collection of cord blood throughout the United States. The idea has been slow getting started, but the eventual hope is to collect enough cord blood so that anyone who needs a blood or bone marrow transplant can find a good match. Meanwhile, private cord blood companies make it possible today for parents to bank their newborns' cord blood as insurance that a good match will be available should their babies ever get sick as Nathan did. When the baby is born, a doctor extracts the cord blood from the umbilical cord, places it in a collection bag, and then sends it to a storage facility, where it is labeled and frozen against the day the baby may need it. Other nonprofit banks collect cord blood from donors and make it available to people who need transplants but have no donor match. Although the chance that a child will need his or her own cord blood is rare, sometimes these stored cord blood cells have even helped family members.

## Life from a Cord Blood Bank

When Brandyn Orr was two years old, he developed leukemia. For three years doctors treated him with chemotherapy and radiation, and the treatments seemed to work. After Brandyn turned six, however, he relapsed, and the cancer came back. Brandyn's cord blood had not been saved when he was born, but by the time his little brother was born, his parents had learned about cord blood banks and saved little Devyn's cord blood. Devyn's cord blood was waiting, frozen at the cord blood bank, when Brandyn's cancer returned. Devyn was a perfect match for Brandyn, but he was only four months old, too young to donate his bone marrow to his brother. His cord blood, however, would save Brandyn's life.

Like Nathan, Brandyn was given strong chemotherapy to kill his own blood cells. Then Devyn's cord blood was transplanted into Brandyn. In 2004, five years after the transplant, Brandyn was still perfectly healthy and cancer-free. Says the boys' mother, "Thank God I didn't have to go through searching the donor registries. I saw so many patients in the transplant ward who suffered through many more complications than Brandyn because they didn't have matching stem cells within their own family."[25]

Cord blood stem cells can be an extremely valuable treatment for blood diseases that require blood stem cell transplants. If these transplants are performed by reputable doctors, they save lives. Many desperate people,

## Let's Get Together

In the United States, there are about twenty cord blood banks where cord blood is stored. Altogether, these banks hold about fifty thousand units of frozen cord blood. That is not enough to meet the needs of people who could be helped with cord blood transplants that are a good match. Scientists estimate that at least one hundred thousand more units are needed, but collection of cord blood is expensive. Many private cord blood banks cannot afford to increase their supply. They also cannot afford registering all the blood so that people know what types are available. People who need a match for a transplant have to search all these banks separately because a national registry has not been established.

Congress appointed an advisory group, the Institute of Medicine, to look into these problems and make recommendations about what should be done. The Institute of Medicine suggested in 2005 that Congress increase funding for cord blood collection and establish a national cord blood coordinating center where doctors and patients could easily discover if a match existed for them in any bank in the country. The institute also suggested that new parents be educated in the value of donated cord blood and asked to donate it to save others.

*A technician at a cord blood bank places boxes of cord blood in a subzero storage tank.*

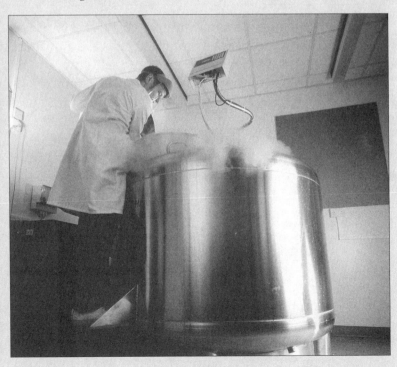

## Saving Rats

Dr. Robert J. Henning and his scientific team at the University of South Florida and James A. Haley Veterans' Hospital experimented with cord blood stem cells and rats. In 2005, they reported that they had helped rats that had heart attacks by using stem cells from cord blood. A heart attack kills heart muscle cells when the blood supply is cut off from the heart. Henning's team injected cord blood stem cells into the rats' hearts about one hour after their heart attacks. After about four months, the rats' hearts showed very little muscle damage and were able to pump blood at near-normal strength.

Henning is not sure how the cord blood cells prevented heart damage and helped the rats to heal after their heart attacks, but he and his team are doing more research so they can understand exactly what happened. He says perhaps the blood cells differentiated into heart cells. Normally, blood stem cells cannot give rise to heart cells, but the immaturity of cord blood cells may make such differentiation possible. Henning also theorizes that the stem cells may have secreted growth chemicals that made the rats' hearts repair themselves. He is searching for the answer with more experiments. If he can learn how cord blood stem cells work in rats, he hopes to be able to apply this treatment to healing people who have heart attacks.

however, hear about how wonderful cord blood seems to be and believe that these cells are a miracle cure. No stem cell treatment is yet a miracle cure, and much more research is needed before the full promise of stem cells becomes a reality. Unfortunately, some unscrupulous people have taken advantage of suffering individuals who hope that cord blood stem cells can cure them.

## When Cord Blood Stem Cells Fail

Tom Hill was one of those desperate people. Hill, fifty-five years old in 2002, had amyotrophic lateral sclerosis (ALS), also known as Lou Gehrig's disease. This horrible disease attacks the brain and nervous system so that muscles no longer work. The individual becomes helplessly crippled and slowly dies. There is no treatment for Lou Gehrig's disease. When news of the discovery of human stem cells was released, Hill was one of many people who had hope where there had never been hope before. Even though no research or progress in stem cell therapy had been made, he believed stem cells could save him. In 2003, he read about stem cell research and scribbled a note to his wife: "It's worth a try."[26]

Hill found a company on the Internet that advertised that it could cure many different diseases with cord blood stem cells. The company claimed that it could inject these cells into the body, the cells would migrate to the site of the disease, and then the cells would start to grow, replacing the body's diseased cells with new, healthy ones. Hill believed the company, flew to Canada, paid thousands of dollars, and had cord blood cells injected into his bloodstream and his belly. The injections did Hill no good. Reputable doctors knew that the company was not helping people and refused to work for it. Finally, the U.S. and Canadian governments accused the company of fraud and shut down its operations. Overseas, companies such as the one that took Hill's money are still operating, but they are not curing anyone. Hill died in 2004, having never been helped by his cord blood stem cell injections.

Irving Weissman was very upset to learn how people were being misled about stem cell therapies. "It's totally disgusting,"[27] he said. Even though cord blood stem cells are valuable treatments for some diseases, they are not magical. They do not seek out diseased organs or cells when injected into the bloodstream or stomach. Even if these stem cells did find their way to the nervous system of someone with Lou Gehrig's disease, they could not become nerve cells. Cord blood stem cells do not automatically change from one kind of cell, such as a blood cell, to another kind of cell. Cord blood stem cells are immature, but they are still adult stem cells. Adult stem cells are not pluripotent. They are multipotent. So they can become any kind of blood cell but not any kind of body cell. Stem cell research has not yet advanced far enough to help people such as Hill, but scientists at the

University of Minnesota's Cancer Center are studying ways to improve treatments of blood diseases with
cord blood stem cells.

## Cord Blood Research in Minnesota

Under the direction of Dr. John Wagner, the cord
blood stem cell research at the cancer center is focused
on making cord blood stem cell transplants safer and
more successful than ever before. Wagner knows that
cord blood stem cells are no miracle cure. He has
learned that the success of cord blood transplants
depends largely on how many stem cells are available
to be given to the patient. The small number of stem
cells in the umbilical cord makes it difficult to save
many patients. Wagner has also discovered that cord
blood stem cells take much longer to grow a new
blood system for a patient than do the adult stem cells
in a person's own body. Researchers at the University
of Minnesota are working to overcome both these
problems. According to the University's Web site,
"The risk posed by umbilical cord blood is that its
stem cells do take longer than the stem cells of bone
marrow to begin working. Particularly for adults with
small umbilical cord [transplants], it may be twice
as long depending on the cell dose. This time lag is
critical. . . . To overcome the time lag, doctors try to
do with drugs and stem cell expansion what the body
can do naturally."[28]

The Minnesota researchers have made remarkable
progress in solving these problems. They have learned
to separate stem cells from cord blood in the laboratory and produce millions of proliferating stem cells.
With drugs and sterile hospital conditions, they have
learned to help patients' bodies accept cord blood
transplants and to stay healthy until new blood systems can grow. One method that seems promising
involves combining the cord blood from two different umbilical cord donations, even though each may
only partially match the patient's blood. This gives

doctors more cord blood stem cells to use without harming the patient. Wagner also continues to study how to prevent the rejection of stem cell transplants and why and when this rejection happens. The entire cancer center team is working to improve treatments with cord blood stem cells. Wagner says, "The results are very promising, but we're never satisfied. That's why our research program is so broad, deep, and aggressive. We're always looking for better treatment

*Doctor John Wagner saved Molly Nash (left) from a fatal genetic disease by giving her blood drawn from the umbilical cord of her brother Adam (asleep in Wagner's arms).*

tools, better ways to improve survival to the goal of 100 percent."[29]

Cord blood stem cells are a new, exciting therapy for some blood diseases, but stem cell research is just beginning, and no one knows which kinds of stem cells will someday prove to be the most valuable. As research continues with umbilical cord stem cells, other scientists are studying adult stem cells from adult bodies and opening up treatment opportunities that were never before imagined.

# CHAPTER 4

# Adult Stem Cell Therapies

Except for the hematopoietic stem cells from bone marrow, adult stem cells are difficult for scientists to use in medical therapies. Adult stem cells are hard to identify and isolate, do not grow easily in the laboratory, and often remain inactive instead of turning on to make new cells. Most adult stem cell research has yielded no medical treatments as yet, but stem cells from bone marrow are a different story. They are very active and easily accessible to doctors. Bone marrow stem cells have been used very successfully for treating some blood and bone diseases.

Two major kinds of adult stem cells exist in bone marrow. Hematopoietic stem cells give rise to the eight different kinds of blood cells—red blood cells, white blood cells, platelets, and more. Mesenchymal stem cells differentiate into bone, cartilage, and fibrous connective tissue. Other adult stem cells, as yet unnamed but with blood- and bone-forming abilities, also hide within bone marrow. Of all the stem cells in bone marrow, however, scientists know the most about hematopoietic stem cells.

Hematopoietic stem cells are turned on and active because they must continually replace short-lived blood cells. As science writer Ann B. Parson explains, "With every passing second roughly two million red cells are expiring, and two million others are hurtling

*The sophisticated machinery on the left extracts stem cells directly from this donor's blood. The process makes surgery to retrieve them from the bone marrow unnecessary.*

out of the bone marrow and into circulation to take their place."[30] With such very active stem cells, doctors were able to use bone marrow transplants to treat some blood diseases even before stem cells were discovered. In the 1980s, doctors first used bone marrow transplants to cure people with cancers of the blood. Doctors now know that the reason for this success is that hematopoietic stem cells are transplanted with the marrow. The stem cells are accepted by the patient's own marrow and replace diseased blood cells with healthy ones. Bone marrow transplants are actually stem cell transplants. Since it is so difficult to isolate stem cells,

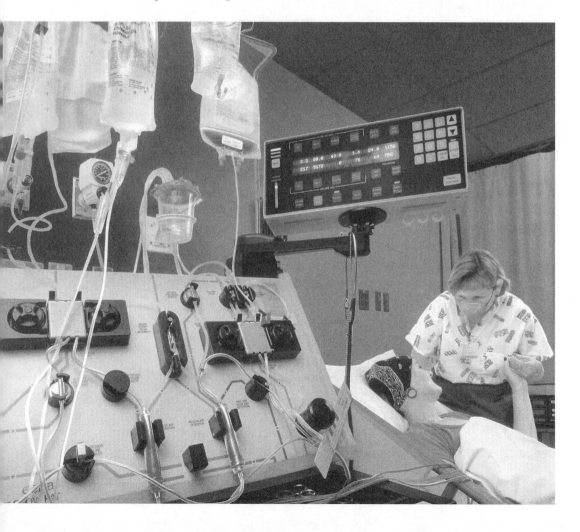

## The Long Road to Health

At St. Jude, as at other transplant hospitals, young people who receive stem cell transplants go through a process that lasts at least one hundred days. First, each patient must be prepared for the transplant with chemotherapy or radiation to kill diseased cells. Antibiotics are given to patients, too, so that they will not have to fight germs while their own immune systems are weak. Once the patient is ready, the transplant itself is performed. It is a quick procedure. The transplant is a fluid, infused into the patient intravenously, with a needle inserted into the vein. It usually takes no longer than a few minutes and causes no pain.

During the several weeks that doctors wait for the transplanted stem cells to travel through the bloodstream to the bone marrow and build a new blood system, the patient is carefully protected from infections. All food must be sterile. Patients wear special masks to protect them from breathing germs when they leave their own rooms and walk around the hospital. When they are ready to leave the hospital, patients move with their families to nearby living facilities, such as Ronald McDonald House. They still wear their masks there and wash their hands often. During all this time, doctors watch for infections, look for signs of graft-versus-host disease, and keep checking blood counts to see if the stem cells are doing their jobs. Once the blood counts show a normal blood system, the patient is finally ready to go home and live a normal life, returning to the hospital only for periodic checkups.

whole bone marrow is often used when a stem cell transplant is necessary.

## Stem Cells and Cancer

One of the places where research with adult stem cells from bone marrow has been the most successful is St. Jude Children's Research Hospital in Memphis, Tennessee. Since the 1960s, when only 4 percent of children with leukemia lived, great progress has been made with this blood cancer. Today, more than 80 percent of children with leukemia survive, thanks to hematopoietic stem cell transplants. St. Jude's goal, however, is to cure all diseases that can be treated with the adult stem cells that come from human bone marrow.

To treat diseases of the blood, doctors at St. Jude transplant bone marrow stem cells into the sick child. These transplants, sometimes called "grafts," come from donors whose antigens match the patient's as closely as possible. Ideally, all six antigens in the bone marrow must match. Otherwise, the transplant will fail when the child's body rejects and attacks the donor cells. Conversely, the donated marrow cells can attack the patient's cells in a process called graft-versus-host disease. The immune system factors that cause this disease are T cells, which occur in the bone marrow of all people. For about half the children at St. Jude who need a transplant, no good donor match can be found. These children cannot be treated with transplants. Half the time, however, someone in the child's family or an unrelated donor is found to be a good match. Then, a bone marrow transplant is a lifesaving treatment.

Just as was done in Nathan Salley's case, doctors at St. Jude use chemotherapy to kill the leukemia cells and then transplant donated bone marrow into the patient. The stem cells grow into a new healthy blood system. Researchers have also developed a way to use the patient's own stem cells for some transplants so that the patient has a perfect match. This method can be used only with a few kinds of cancers, when a child is in remission or the cancer has already been destroyed. If doctors believe there is a possibility the cancer will return, they can extract some of the child's own bone marrow, freeze it, and store it. Then, if the cancer does come back, the child can receive a transplant of his or her own stem cells.

## Stem Cells and Brittle Bone Disease

St. Jude researchers have also used mesenchymal stem cells from bone marrow to treat bone diseases. In 1997, Dr. Ed Horwitz used an injection of bone marrow stem cells to treat a boy with osteogenesis imperfecta, or brittle bone disease. As Jacob Menzel was being born, his bones began to break. A mistake in the DNA code in his genes had caused him to be born with brittle bone disease. Jacob's bones fractured with the slight-

est movement and could not grow normally. Children with brittle bone disease remain very tiny, and their bodies become deformed. Sometimes, they even die from this disease. When Jacob was born, no treatments existed to help him. By the time Jacob was three, however, Horwitz realized that bone stem cells, as well as blood-forming cells, hid in bone marrow. He gave Jacob injections of whole bone marrow in the hope that the mesenchymal cells would grow healthy bone. Jacob was not cured, but the stem cells did go to work in his bone marrow and begin growing new bone. Jacob was healthier, and his bones appeared stronger. Jacob's mother remarked, "The stem cell infusions definitely helped. The science just makes sense: you

*A seven-year-old boy with brittle bone disease is made honorary police chief for a day. A stem cell transplant could potentially cure his disease.*

introduce cells into somebody's body, and the body accepts those cells."[31]

Horwitz hoped the stem cells would continue to grow in Jacob's body and make new bone cells, but for unknown reasons, they stopped working after a while. Horwitz gave Jacob a second transplant and then a third. Each transplant helped. Jacob was able to go to school and play with friends, but no transplant had a lasting effect. Horwitz and other St. Jude scientists needed to figure out why the bone stem cells did not keep working. They wanted to cure osteogenesis imperfecta, once and for all. Horwitz says,

> This is an exciting new approach because it shows for the first time that mesenchymal cell engraftment has the potential to correct inherited disorders. We believe patients with bone disorders who are treated with this approach will ultimately have a much greater chance of enhanced life since we are treating the underlying problem that causes the disorder, not just treating the symptoms.[32]

First, researchers at St. Jude would have to do more work. They figured out how to separate mesenchymal stem cells from all the billions of cells in bone marrow. Then Horwitz tried a transplant with these stem cells in a second child with brittle bone disease. This child also got better, but again the bone growth did not last. "We'd love to be able to give them one treatment and have them cured," said Horwitz. "But we're not there yet."[33]

## Trying Again . . . and Again

Horwitz and his team kept experimenting, trying to understand which stem cells grew bone most reliably. In 2004, they discovered another stem cell in bone marrow. It was a new cell with no name that seemed to differentiate into both bone and blood cells. In 2005, Horwitz tried a transplant with this newly isolated cell for another child with brittle bone disease, eight-year-old Molly Hammond. Luckily, Molly had a sis-

## A Cell Therapy Product

At the ends of the two bones that come together to form the knee is a spongy protective material called cartilage. Cartilage cushions the ends of the bones, and if it is damaged, the joint becomes painful, swollen, and difficult to move. Carticel is an adult stem cell treatment to replace this torn or damaged cartilage. The Carticel process involves extracting some normal cartilage from the patient's knee, isolating the adult stem cells, and then growing the cartilage-producing stem cells in the laboratory. When millions of cartilage cells have been grown, a doctor surgically places them back into the patient's knee. There, they implant themselves, continue to multiply, and make new, healthy cartilage. Carticel treatment for wounded cartilage was first used in 1997. By 2004, it had helped ten thousand people. Although not every patient is cured, most report that they are very much improved and can walk without pain.

ter whose bone marrow was a perfect match. Horwitz took the donated bone marrow, extracted the new cells along with mesenchymal cells, and grafted the stem cells into Molly's bone marrow. Horowitz is still waiting to see if these cells will last in Molly's body. She continues to need a wheelchair, but she is already healthier and stronger. When Molly was born, her mother had to carry her around on a pillow so she would not break Molly's bones by accident. Molly's mother is no longer afraid to touch her daughter. "The transplants at St. Jude have helped Molly tremendously," says Molly's mom. "Her fracture rates have decreased, and she's grown. I think it's everything that St. Jude has done with this treatment that has made her who she is today." With the continuing research at St. Jude, Molly and her mother are looking forward to the future. Molly's mother adds, "We have hopes that Molly will walk one day."[34]

Horwitz wants Molly to walk, too. He is back in the lab, trying to find the chemical or medicine that will force adult stem cells to graft successfully in the bone marrow, turn themselves on, and keep growing. Someday, he wants to be able to cure all children with brittle bone disease. He says, "To find a cure for OI

*At age five, Austin Jones received a stem cell transplant in an effort to cure him of his sickle-cell disease, a crippling disorder caused by irregularly shaped blood cells (inset).*

[osteogenesis imperfecta], you're going to need to find a cell that can continually make bone, get it inside the bone, and then find a way to make it happen. Now how can we make it happen at will? That's what we're exploring in the laboratory right now."[35]

## Stem Cells and Sickle-Cell Disease

Meanwhile, other researchers at St. Jude are using stem cells to help children with another devastating disease called sickle-cell disease. Sickle-cell is a painful, crippling disease in which many blood cells are the wrong shape. They are crescent-shaped instead of round and therefore get stuck as they move through the blood vessels. They can block the vessels, causing strokes and seizures. Not only do children with sickle-cell disease suffer terrible episodes of pain, but the clogged blood vessels can damage organs and cause death if the disease is left untreated. Sickle-cell is an inherited disease that most commonly affects African Americans. Although medical treatments, such as blood transfusions, exist for sickle-cell disease, there was no cure for a long time. Doctors at St. Jude changed that. They have treated more than two hundred children with sickle-cell disease using bone marrow transplants of stem cells.

Shandel Narcisse, who lived on the Caribbean island of St. Lucia, had sickle-cell disease and suffered

# Genetic Disease

An inherited disease is caused by a mistake in a person's genetic coding. This mistake could have been passed on to the individual from parents or could have happened when the embryonic cells were dividing. Such mistakes are called mutations. These genetic accidents happen because cells have to recopy their DNA before they divide, and the recopying process can cause errors. Scientists explain that a gene is like the word in a message with coding instructions, and a mutation is a typographical error.

In his book *Jacob's Ladder*, scientist Henry Gee explains how the giant human book of genetic coding can go wrong. In his example, he explains that DNA forms the letters in genetic words. The code, which must be read in groups of three letters each, is a DNA string of instructions like this:

DIDYOUSEEOURDADJIMANDHISBIGFATCATMAX.

If the letters are broken into groups of three and read as words, they make sense:

DID YOU SEE OUR DAD JIM AND HIS BIG FAT CAT MAX.

If an extra letter is thrown into this sequence, it is like a DNA mistake that occurs as the cell is duplicating its DNA and preparing to divide. A little piece of extra DNA is hooked by mistake to the message:

DIDYOUSEEXOURDADJIMANDHISBIGFATCATMAX.

Now, when the code is broken into groups of three, nothing makes sense:

DID YOU SEE XOU RDA DJI MAN DHI SBI GFA TCA TMA X.

Just one small addition affected the whole sentence and made it all wrong. This is what happens when a genetic mutation takes place. It is a tiny error, but it can cause a terrible disease in which an entire chemical direction in the body does not work. Gee says that DNA misprints like these are the cause of many congenital diseases.

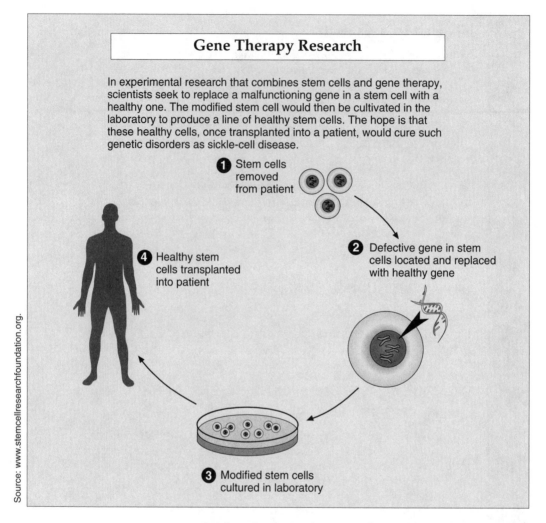

**Gene Therapy Research**

In experimental research that combines stem cells and gene therapy, scientists seek to replace a malfunctioning gene in a stem cell with a healthy one. The modified stem cell would then be cultivated in the laboratory to produce a line of healthy stem cells. The hope is that these healthy cells, once transplanted into a patient, would cure such genetic disorders as sickle-cell disease.

**1** Stem cells removed from patient

**2** Defective gene in stem cells located and replaced with healthy gene

**4** Healthy stem cells transplanted into patient

**3** Modified stem cells cultured in laboratory

Source: www.stemcellresearchfoundation.org.

a stroke by the time he was four. Shandel's mother was desperate to help him. She said, "Shandel's doctor told me that if he kept on getting seizures and strokes, he would die. The doctor said we had to find a way to get Shandel a bone marrow transplant. But they don't do them at home; we would have to go to the United States."[36] In 2000, Shandel and his family went to St. Jude. Doctors tested Shandel's brother Randel and discovered that he was a perfect match for a bone marrow transplant. Shandel's own bone marrow, which produced sickle cells, was replaced by his brother's healthy cells. Because Shandel was lucky enough to have a donor match from his brother, he was cured.

Four years after his transplant, Shandel was a healthy, active eight-year-old. His mother said, "Every day I see how Shandel's improving. I thank God for that. In the beginning, I'd have to hold Shandel's hand and walk slowly. But now I don't have to hold his hand; he's always running!"[37] Sadly, many children with sickle-cell disease have no donor match. St. Jude researchers are trying to solve that problem.

## Sorting Cells and Saving Lives

Dr. Rupert Handgretinger is the director of stem cell transplantation at St. Jude. Since most parents are willing to be donors for their children, he is researching ways to use the parents' bone marrow and prevent it from causing graft-versus-host disease. Because children inherit half their genetic material from each parent, each child has three antigens in common with each parent. Three for three is not a good enough match to prevent graft-versus-host disease.

In the laboratory, Handgretinger invented a new method to separate the cells in bone marrow. He figured out a chemical way to magnetize stem cells and sort them from the rest of the bone marrow in a special magnetized chamber. Handgretinger's method now makes it possible for parents to donate bone marrow for transplantation, even without a perfect antigen match, because pure stem cells are less likely to be rejected than whole marrow. Handgretinger explains,

> We developed a method whereby we can process billions and billions of cells and pick out only the stem cells, leaving the rest behind. You'll never find a more motivated donor than the mom or dad of the patient. And you have the donor sitting at the patient's bedside every day. If you need a second transplantation, you don't have to do a donor search, because it's easy to find that donor.[38]

Next, Handgretinger developed a way to magnetize T cells and pull them away from the rest of the marrow. Without T cells, donated bone marrow cannot cause graft-versus-host disease. Handgretinger hopes that this method will help sickle-cell patients and other sick children with no good donor match. He says, "We can never stop doing this kind of research until we improve the survival rates to 100 percent."[39] Handgretinger's procedure is very new. Human trials with this treatment were to begin in late 2005.

## Stem Cells and Gene Therapy

Dr. Derek Persons, another researcher at St. Jude, is experimenting with a different treatment for sickle-cell disease. His research in the laboratory combines stem cells with gene therapy. Explains Persons, "A possibility we are studying is to take the patient's own blood stem cells, to correct them and to place them back into the body."[40] Persons wants to locate the gene in a patient's stem cell that causes sickle-cell disease, remove it, and insert a normal gene in its place. Then he would put this cured stem cell back into the patient's bone marrow. There, the stem cell would have the DNA information to give rise to normal blood cells instead of sickle cells. The technique has already been tried successfully with mice, improving their blood and health.

Persons's team is not ready to try the treatment in sick children. To put a healthy gene into a stem cell, Persons has to use a virus as a carrier because viruses are able to penetrate cells and change the genetic information. Although Persons uses viruses made harmless in the laboratory, he is still not sure that these viruses will not cause sickness in people. Gene therapy with adult stem cells is still in the future, but if it works, it will mean permanent cures for many genetic bone marrow diseases.

Adult stem cells from bone marrow have led to very successful medical treatments, but many scientists believe that pluripotent stem cells have even greater potential for conquering diseases. As Persons says about bone marrow stem cells, "You never know where the answer will come from."[41] Instead of studying adult stem cells, scientists in other laboratories search for answers with embryonic stem cell research.

# CHAPTER 5

# Using Embryonic Stem Cells

Embryonic stem cell research is a quest for cures of diseases for which adult stem cells seem unsuited. No human treatments with embryonic stem cells have yet been successful, because the research is so new, but this research is both tantalizing and meaningful for what the results may someday mean for human medical treatment.

## Mice and Stem Cell Lines

At present, almost all the research experiments with embryonic stem cells are performed on mice. Laboratory mice are ideal creatures for experiments with embryonic stem cell treatments because mice are genetically similar to people. Scientists estimate that they have 80 to 95 percent of the same genes that humans have. As science writer Gina Kolata observes, "A mouse, in fact, is essentially a human with its genes rearranged."[42] Scientists have learned the function of many mouse genes, pinpointed where they are on mouse chromosomes, and identified which genetic mistakes cause different diseases. Researchers have also become very adept at growing mouse embryonic stem cells into stem cell lines for experiments.

Stem cell lines are laboratory dishes of proliferating embryonic stem cells that do not differentiate. To make a stem cell line, a scientist first flushes a three-day-old mouse embryo from a pregnant mouse, just as Gail Martin did when she first discovered embryonic stem cells. Next, the scientist carefully retrieves the stem cells from the inner mass of the blastocyst. The cells are placed in a nutrient bath in a petri dish and allowed to divide and grow. There, they give rise to millions of unspecialized embryonic stem cells that can be used for experiments. It is from mouse embryonic stem cell lines that researchers have learned the most about how to treat disease.

*Embryonic stem cell cultures are stored in an incubator at the Center for Genome Research at Edinburgh University in Scotland.*

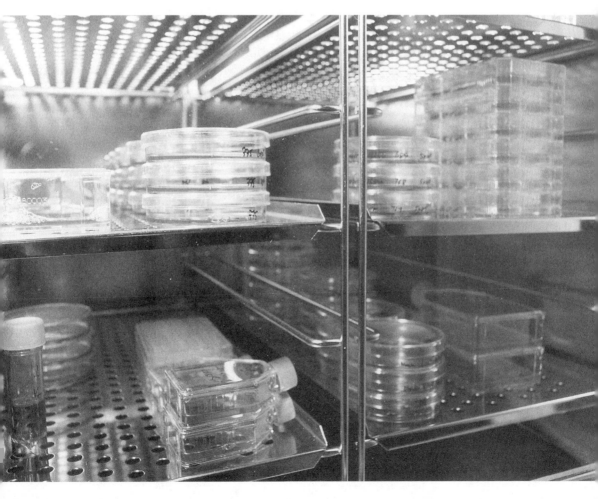

## "Knockout Mice"

To learn how to cure disease with stem cells, however, scientists need mice that have human diseases. Such mice live in thousands of scientific laboratories. They are called "knockout mice." Knockout mice are created by removing or knocking out a gene from a mouse embryo. The embryo is then allowed to develop. When it is born, the cells in its body are missing this gene and its coding instructions. When the mouse mates and has babies of its own, those babies, too, have defective genetic instructions. Now scientists have a strain of mice carrying this problem. If the scientists knocked out a gene that was necessary to prevent an inherited disease, the knockout mouse will have that disease, and all its babies will inherit it. Knockout mice help scientists understand how missing DNA information in genes causes disease. Mario Capecchi, who created the first knockout mouse in 1989, explained, "It allowed us to define exactly what a gene was doing in the life of an organism."[43]

Knockout mice can be developed that have human diseases so that scientists can experiment with stem cell lines to find a way to cure them. At the Jackson Laboratory in Bar Harbor, Maine, scientists have developed more than eight hundred different strains of mice, named for the type of disease they carry. "Shiver" mice have a genetic mistake that causes the coating around their nerves, called myelin, to be abnormal. "Twitcher" mice twitch and jerk. "Stargazers" have a muscle and nerve problem that makes them continually throw their heads up. "Dwarf" mice are missing the normal growth gene. Other strains of mice have diabetes, cancer, obesity, heart disease, or no T cells to protect them from germs. Embryonic stem cell researchers can order any of these mouse strains from Jackson Laboratory and experiment with curing their diseases.

## The Bubble Boy

The original bubble boy, David Vetter, was born in 1971 with a disease known as severe combined immune deficiency syndrome (SCIDS). He had inherited a genetic mistake that meant his body had no ability to resist any germs or sickness. Most such children do not survive, but from the minute he was born, David was kept isolated in a sterile environment so that he would never be exposed to any kind of germ. The plastic bubble that David lived in was large. It had room for a bed, toys, a playroom, and eating facilities. The sides of the bubble were equipped with thick rubber gloves so that adults could reach in to David, care for him, and even hug him, without skin-to-skin contact. When David went home from the hospital, he lived in a bubble set up for him there.

David's parents and doctors hoped that a cure would be found for SCIDS that would free him from his isolated life. Doctors searched for a donor match in the hope that a bone marrow transplant could cure David and release him from the bubble. For years, no perfect donor match could be found. Finally, in 1983, doctors decided to risk using donated bone marrow from David's sister, even though she was only a partial match.

For a few months, David survived and seemed to be accepting the transplant. For a couple of weeks, he even was able to leave his bubble and live in a regular hospital room. Then, suddenly, he became very ill. Although doctors had not known it, David's sister had once had a mild sickness, the Epstein-Barr virus. It had not made her ill at all, but the virus hid in her bloodstream and bone marrow. Once released into David's body, the virus caused a severe cancer. He died on February 22, 1984, when he was twelve years old.

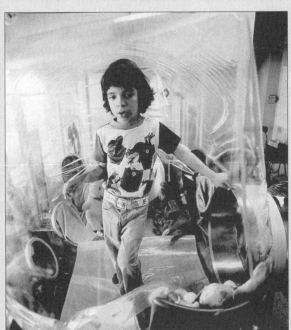

*Born with a genetic disorder that left him with no immunity against disease, David Vetter had to live his short life inside a sterile bubble.*

## A Knockout Mouse Treatment

At the Whitehead Institute for Biomedical Research, in Massachusetts, George Daley and Rudolf Jaenisch used knockout mice with destroyed immune systems for their embryonic stem cell research. First the scientists took a skin cell from a diseased mouse's tail. Then they removed the nucleus of the skin cell, with all its DNA information, and added it to a mouse egg. Next, the egg was grown to the blastocyst stage and its embryonic stem cells removed. Then Daley and Jaenisch added the gene that provides instructions for a healthy immune system to the ES cells. They grew the corrected ES cells into a stem cell line in the lab. This stem cell line now had genes identical to those of the sick mouse but with a healthy gene for coding the growth of immune system cells. The scientists treated the ES cell line in a petri dish with certain nutritive chemicals that made the cells differentiate into hematopoietic immune system cells. At last, they were ready to inject the cells into the diseased mouse. Both scientists were excited to observe that the mouse got better. It was not cured, but its immune system improved. Daley said, "Though the immune system wasn't completely restored, there was enough improvement to predict that a comparable result in humans would translate into significant clinical benefit."[44]

This experiment marked the first time that embryonic stem cells had been used successfully to even partially cure a disease. Helping a mouse with a genetic immune system problem was important because people also have immune deficiency diseases. One severe problem is sometimes called "bubble boy disease." It is named for David Vetter, a boy born in 1971 with no immune system. Having no immune system meant that any germ that other people carried harmlessly would have killed him. In order to keep David alive, he was raised in a large, sterile, plastic bubble that protected him from any contact with the outside world. Daley

## Cell Signaling

When embryonic stem cells are grouped together, they send chemical signals to each other that help control how they differentiate. Generally, cells that are clumped together become the same kind of body cells. Cells in one group, for example, become heart cells; another cluster becomes brain cells. This signaling occurs naturally in the developing embryo, but it also happens in petri dishes in the laboratory. Cells in different areas of the petri dish clump together and spontaneously signal each other, just because they are touching. They differentiate together into the same kind of cells. This is the phenomenon that scientists want to be able to control. If they can learn what the chemical signals are and how they are initiated, then experimenters will be able to mimic the signals and tell stem cells to become any desired kind of body cell.

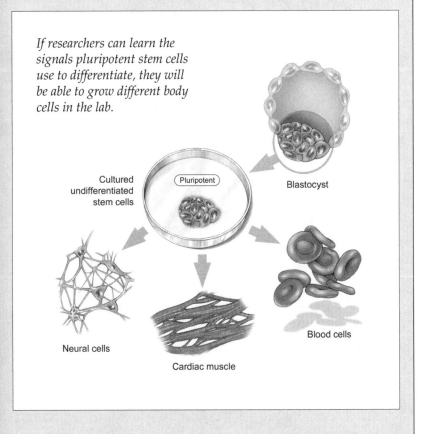

*If researchers can learn the signals pluripotent stem cells use to differentiate, they will be able to grow different body cells in the lab.*

Cultured undifferentiated stem cells

Pluripotent

Blastocyst

Neural cells

Cardiac muscle

Blood cells

said about his mouse experiment, "This was a mouse model of the bubble boy disease. . . . As with many firsts, it was not 100 percent effective. But it at least convinced us that with technology available today, we could put this into practice."[45]

*A researcher injects a culture of stem cells into the spinal cord of a paralyzed rat.*

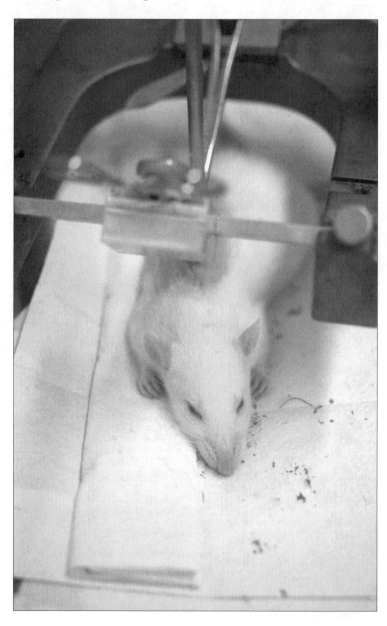

## ES Cells for Diabetes

Daley is not the only scientist excited by the potential of ES cell research. Other researchers have explored cures for diabetes. Type 1 diabetes is a kind of immune system disease in which the body's immune cells mistakenly attack the insulin-making cells in the pancreas. Without insulin, the body cannot control the amount of sugar in the blood. Insulin-producing cells are called beta cells, and once they die, they are not replaced. As far as scientists know, the pancreas has no adult stem cells. At Stanford University in California, Dr. Seung K. Kim and his scientific team used mouse embryonic stem cells to treat diabetic mice. Kim used special chemicals to make his stem cell line differentiate into beta cells. Then he grafted some of these cells into the mice. Not all the beta cells survived, but about 10 percent of them began making insulin in the mice's pancreases. That was enough to keep the mice alive, but not to cure them. "This is one step in the right direction,"[46] said Kim. He had proved that embryonic stem cells could be grown into pancreatic cells in the lab and then used as a diabetes treatment—in mice, at least.

Kim and other stem cell researchers continue to explore treatments for diabetic mice because curing mice could mean a cure for diabetes in people. People like eleven-year-old Catherine look forward to the day that knockout mice point the way to a human cure. Catherine once described her life with diabetes this way: "It's still hard to get used to diabetes. It's a nuisance to do my glucose levels before every meal. I hate injections and I have to have two a day! I have to eat six meals a day, even if I am not hungry and when I go to a birthday party, I can eat a few sweets, but I can't pig out!"[47] Knockout mice and embryonic stem cell research could change that. People like Catherine are why scientists keep working to understand stem cells. So far, though, they do not know enough even to cure mice, much less people.

## Cured Before Birth

In 2004, Robert Benezra and Diego Fraidenraich at Memorial Sloan-Kettering Cancer Center in New York used ES cells to cure mice with genetic heart defects before the mice were even born. The mother mouse carried a DNA mistake that caused her babies to be born with malfunctioning hearts. The heart defects were so severe that untreated baby mice born with this defect always died. When the mother mouse was pregnant, Benezra and Fraidenraich carefully injected fifteen ES cells into each tiny embryo in her womb. The ES cells did not cure all the babies, but 50 percent of them were born with normal hearts. Not only did the ES cells differentiate into normal heart cells, they also stopped the defective stem cells in the embryos from differentiating into defective heart cells. The researchers believed that their ES cells apparently sent chemical signals to the defective stem cells that made them repair themselves. The baby mice were born with normal, healthy hearts that showed no signs of a genetic coding mistake. Before this experiment took place, scientists did not know that healthy ES cells could signal their neighbors and restore them to normal functioning.

## ES Cells and Spinal Cord Injuries

Still, scientists have accomplished remarkable feats, even with injuries that were once considered hopeless. In 1999, Dr. John McDonald decided to see what he could do with embryonic stem cells for mice with spinal cord injuries. Spinal cord injuries cause paralysis and involve very complicated cell damage. Several kinds of nerve cells are damaged, and no treatment has ever been found. McDonald grew a stem line of mouse embryonic cells and figured out a way to differentiate the ES cells into nerve cells. They were only one kind of nerve cell, but he tried injecting them into the paralyzed mice. The mice had been paralyzed for nine days and could not move their hindquarters at all. One month after the nerve cell injection, the treatment enabled the mice to move their legs and to stand up. The myelin coating on their nerves had been partially replaced.

They could not walk and their movements were uncoordinated but they had definitely improved. McDonald was encouraged even though the mice were not cured. He said, "Their walking certainly wasn't normal. But this functional recovery was especially encouraging because the cells were transplanted nine days after the spinal cord injury—a time period that had not yet been explored."[48] McDonald was pleased because the improvement might mean that people with such injuries could be treated, even months after they were injured.

McDonald's ultimate goal is to help people with spinal cord injuries, who are also missing the myelin coating that insulates the communication nerves in the spinal cord. He once explained, "We are using these cells to create new circuits and rejuvenate damaged circuits within the cord, replacing cells that were lost during or after injury. We hope that such transplants—and the knowledge of mechanisms gained by such transplants—will provide meaningful gains in independence for people with spinal cord injury, such as regaining bowel or bladder control or improving the use of the arms and legs."[49]

## ES Cells and Lou Gehrig's Disease

A year after McDonald's experiment, John Gearhart joined with Dr. Douglas Kerr at Johns Hopkins to try another experiment with paralyzed mice. These mice had been given a virus that caused a spinal cord disease like the ALS or Lou Gehrig's disease that affects people. Gearhart and Kerr injected embryonic stem cells into the spinal fluid that surrounds the spinal cord. They hoped that the ES cells would travel to the cord, differentiate, and begin repairs. After one month, they saw no change and thought the experiment was a failure. Another month went by. Then one day, Kerr reported, "We first saw a flicker of movement, then [movement in] a second limb, then the flexing of a hind limb."[50]

The scientists were thrilled. Slowly, eleven of the eighteen paralyzed mice improved, and some were even able to walk. The scientists made a videotape of their walking mice to prove to the world that embryonic stem cell research worked and could help paralyzed people some day, too.

## Human ES Cell Research

Mouse embryonic stem cells continue to teach valuable medical lessons, but they are not the same as human embryonic stem cells. Even though human ES cells are easier to grow into stem cell lines than are adult stem cells, scientists still did not know how to make them differentiate reliably into the body cells they wanted. If human treatments were to be developed, scientists had to experiment with human ES cells and learn to manipulate them.

*Scientist Michael West, of Advanced Cell Technology, inserts ES cell cultures into petri dishes during research into the development of cell therapies to treat disease.*

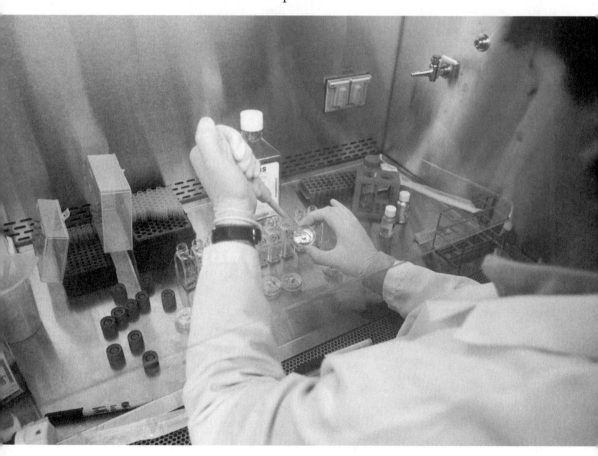

Research with people was much too dangerous, but scientists could grow human embryonic stem cells from in vitro clinics' leftover embryos. In petri dishes, scientists could grow ES cells from blastocysts, discover how human ES cells specialize into different kinds of body cells, and someday use that knowledge to treat human diseases. The major thrust of human ES cell research has been to make embryonic stem cells differentiate into desired body cells in the laboratory. Scientists at the University of Wisconsin–Madison are learning how to direct this human ES cell specialization.

## From ES Cells to Heart Cells

In 2003, Wisconsin scientist Timothy Kamp was able to grow the three major types of human heart muscle cells from an embryonic stem cell line in his laboratory. Kamp says, "Understanding that there is potential to get these different types of heart cells is exciting. The more we learn about these different cells—how they become different cell types, and how we can enrich these different cell types, the closer we'll get to using embryonic stem cells as a source for cell therapy for various forms of heart disease."[51]

Enrichment, or the right nutrition, for specializing stem cells was a tricky problem for scientists. They needed to learn exactly what chemicals or signals in the body directed the specialization of stem cells into heart cells, blood cells, liver cells, and so forth. As they experimented, they learned just the right combinations of nutritional chemical bath, temperature, and environment to grow different cell types. As scientist David Gardner once said about growing stem cells, "We learned from mom that she provides different nutrients for different developmental stages."[52] Vitamins and chemicals that imitated the natural conditions in the womb were critical if differentiation was to occur in petri dishes in the laboratory.

## From ES Cells to Nerve Cells

Years of effort were necessary before Wisconsin researcher Su-Chan Zhang found the right bath to grow nerve cells from human ES cells. Scientists had grown mouse nerve cells long before, but Zhang found that growth of human nerve cells was much more difficult. As he comments, "You need to teach the [embryonic stem cells] to change step by step, where each step has different conditions and a strict window of time. Otherwise, it just won't work."[53] Finally, in 2005, his work succeeded. He had grown brain cells that control movement, called motor nerve cells, in his laboratory, and they were still alive three months later.

Zhang's work showed that mouse experiments did not always help in human research. Mouse nerve cells had been easy for scientists to grow. The nutrient bath that stimulated them was not complicated. Zhang's human cells needed a completely different mix of nutrients, and nutrients that were changed at different times, in order to specialize reliably. Human ES cell research would be absolutely necessary if treatments for people were ever to become a reality. Zhang says, "We cannot simply translate studies from animals to humans."[54]

Even with Zhang's success, medical treatments for nerve diseases and spinal cord injuries in people are still years away. Scientists need to learn much more from human ES cell research in the laboratory before they can use these cells safely with people. Researchers such as Zhang and Kamp aim for more breakthroughs that will someday lead to human ES cell therapies. Already, they can picture how the cures may come about.

# CHAPTER 6

# Hopeless No More?

Actor Michael J. Fox once described what the symptoms of his Parkinson's disease were like when the medicine he used to control them wore off:

> When I'm "off," the disease has complete authority over my physical being. I'm utterly in its possession. Sometimes there are flashes of function, and I can be effective at performing basic level tasks, certainly feeding and dressing myself (though I'll lean toward loafers and pullover sweaters), as well as any chore calling for more brute force than manual dexterity. In my very worst "off" times I experience the full panoply of classic Parkinson's symptoms: rigidity, shuffling, tremors, lack of balance, diminished motor control, and the insidious cluster of symptoms that make communication—written as well as spoken—difficult and sometimes impossible.[55]

Parkinson's is a cruel and destructive disease of the brain in which the type of brain cells responsible for producing an essential chemical called dopamine die. Without dopamine, the brain cannot coordinate body muscles and movement. People with Parkinson's disease move slowly, shuffle when they walk, and have rigid muscles. They have shaking movements, called tremors, in some body parts, and easily lose their balance. Although doctors can give dopamine medicines that help for a while, over time the medicines stop working. The patient's ability to control his or her body

*During a 1999 Senate hearing, actor Michael J. Fox, who suffers from Parkinson's disease, urges the government to support stem cell research.*

becomes worse and worse. More than a million people in the United States alone have Parkinson's disease.

With Parkinson's disease, as well as many other untreatable diseases, scientists look to the different types of stem cell research for the treatments of the future. Although it will be some time before stem cells yield treatments for the worst diseases and injuries, already scientists can envision the pathway by which their experiments will become the cures that millions of people await.

## Therapeutic Cloning

Research suggests that a technique called therapeutic cloning could be the best treatment for people who have Parkinson's disease. Therapeutic cloning is a method of getting embryonic stem cells that are a match to the patient. It is a complicated process, but it has already been used successfully in animals. First, the scientist would take a human egg and remove its nucleus, which is where all the chemical DNA information is found. Into this enucleated egg, the scientist inserts the nucleus from a cell from the sick person's own body, such as a skin cell. This skin cell nucleus has the chromosomes, genes, and DNA that are unique to that person. The egg, with its new nucleus, can be stimulated to divide and grow, even without fertilization. A chemical or electrical stimulation is often used. Once the egg has grown into a blastocyst, it is now a perfect DNA match to the patient.

The embryonic stem cells are extracted from the laboratory blastocyst and grown into a stem cell line. Then, using already-identified chemicals, the stem cell line would be directed to grow into dopamine-producing nerve cells, called neurons. These neural cells could be transplanted into the correct part of the brain of the Parkinson's patient, where they would integrate with the existing nerve cells, produce dopamine, and cure the patient. The theory of the process is just like the process that uses bone marrow transplants of adult stem cells to help children born with osteogenesis imperfecta. It is a long step, however, from the theory to the reality.

In 2005, scientists in South Korea grew therapeutically cloned ES cells from eleven people with different disabilities and diseases. Each stem cell line is a genetic match for one of the patients, but the researchers have not attempted any medical treatments yet. Most therapeutic cloning treatments have been with animals. Dr. Ron McKay has grown embryonic stem cell lines into dopamine-producing neurons and transplanted them

## Stem Cells and Therapeutic Cloning

In therapeutic cloning, scientists are not copying embryos. What they do is take the genetic material (DNA) from a cell in a patient's body and fuse it with an empty egg cell from a donor. The new cell grows into an embryo that contains stem cells genetically matched to the patient. Researchers believe these cells can be transplanted into a patient to treat an injury or a disease. There is no chance that such a transplant would be rejected or identified as foreign and attacked by the body, because cells created through therapeutic cloning would be derived from the patient, and the immune system would recognize the cells as the patient's own.

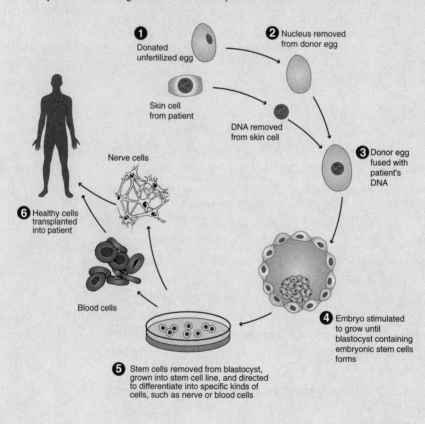

1 Donated unfertilized egg

2 Nucleus removed from donor egg

Skin cell from patient

DNA removed from skin cell

3 Donor egg fused with patient's DNA

Nerve cells

6 Healthy cells transplanted into patient

Blood cells

4 Embryo stimulated to grow until blastocyst containing embryonic stem cells forms

5 Stem cells removed from blastocyst, grown into stem cell line, and directed to differentiate into specific kinds of cells, such as nerve or blood cells

Source: BBC News, July 31, 2000.

into the brains of knockout mice who had Parkinson's disease. The nerve cells made dopamine in the mice's brains, and the condition of the mice improved.

Scientists do not know yet how this method would work in human brains or how to make it safe and effective. They have, however, directed human ES cells to become neural cells in the lab. They have identified the area in the human brain that is most in need of neural cell replacement. If they could inject therapeutically cloned neural cells into human brains, they believe they could greatly improve the symptoms of Parkinson's disease, but more experiments are needed with human cells. McKay says, "This technology is going to matter to Parkinson's patients very soon, but how quickly it will make a big difference to Parkinson's patients, that depends on how the experiments turn out. But within several years it's certain this technology will be important." He adds, "And one other point I think is worth stressing is that it's a general technology. This is not just a Parkinson's-oriented kind of approach. This approach is going to matter in many, many areas of medicine."[56]

## To Move Again

If research continues and questions about human cells can be answered, therapeutic cloning promises hope for many previously incurable problems besides Parkinson's disease. Spinal cord injuries, for example, could benefit from therapeutic cloning. Such injuries, once thought impossible to treat, cause paralysis that extends from the point of the injury down the rest of the body. Actor Christopher Reeve suffered such a devastating injury when he was thrown from a horse in 1995. He described his condition in 2002: "I am paralyzed from the shoulders down and unable to breathe on my own. For the last 7 years, I have not been able to eat, wash, go to the bathroom, or get dressed by myself. Some people are able to accept living with a severe disability. I am not one of them."[57]

Spinal cord injuries involve damage to several kinds of nerve cells. The break in Reeve's spinal cord destroyed the myelin that coated and protected the nerves that carry movement messages from the brain to the muscles. Replacing these cells in human bodies is so complicated that it will be years before scientists perfect the therapeutic cloning treatments that could repair spinal cords. Before he died in 2004, Reeve spoke publicly and wrote extensively of his hope that embryonic stem cell research and therapeutic cloning would one day allow him (and others like him) to walk again.

## A Cell Nuclear Transfer Advance

In May 2005, Woo-Suk Hwang's scientific team at Seoul National University in South Korea reported the first creation of stem cell lines that were therapeutically cloned from human skin cells. The scientists collected donated eggs from eighteen women, removed the nuclei from these eggs, and inserted the nuclei from skin cells taken from patients with spinal cord injuries, diabetes, and immune system diseases. The eggs were chemically stimulated to begin dividing and grown to the blastocyst stage. Then the embryonic stem cells were extracted. Not all the stem cells grew, but from thirty-one blastocysts, eleven stem cell lines succeeded and were perfect genetic matches to the patients. Although medical therapies are still years away, Hwang and his team have brought the world one step closer to using therapeutically cloned stem cells to heal diseases and injuries. Scientists everywhere have hailed Hwang's work as a breakthrough in ES cell research.

*South Korean scientist Woo-Suk Hwang successfully grew the first therapeutically cloned human stem cell lines.*

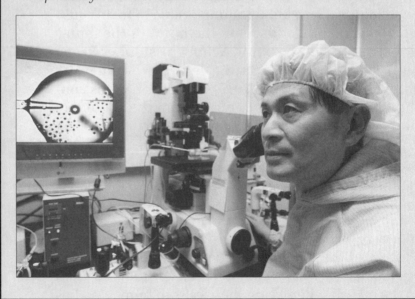

Toward that end, the Christopher Reeve Paralysis Foundation continues to fund and support human ES cell research and therapeutic cloning in the belief that millions of disabled people will benefit.

*Before his death in 2004, actor Christopher Reeve (right) spoke often about the tremendous promise stem cell research and therapeutic cloning hold for people with spinal cord injuries.*

## Is It Cloning?

Therapeutic cloning, however, is as controversial as embryonic stem cell research. The process is the same as the process that would be used to make clones of people. If the therapeutically cloned embryo were implanted into a womb and allowed to grow into a fetus, it would theoretically then be a true copy of the person whose skin cell provided the nucleus for the blastocyst. Almost all scientists reject the idea of human cloning because they think it is unsafe. Cloning attempts with animals have frequently resulted in genetic coding mistakes, leading to premature aging, disease, and suffering for the clone or death for both mother and fetus. Scientists do not know enough to prevent such outcomes in people. Many ethicists and other people oppose cloning, too, believing that there are some things humanity was never meant to do, and cloning is one of them. In 1997, President Bill Clinton called cloning "morally reprehensible."[58]

People against cloning often reject therapeutic cloning, as well. Leon Kass, a professor and presidential adviser, believes it is impossible to draw the line between therapeutic cloning and reproductive cloning. He says, "Once cloned embryos are available in the laboratory having been produced for research nothing prevents them from being used for reproductive purposes."[59] Kass believes that both kinds of cloning should be illegal.

Irving Weissman responds to the moral opposition to therapeutic cloning by pointing out that transferring a nucleus to make stem cell treatments is not the same as reproductive cloning. He once declared, "On my side, I say, if you deny this research, hundreds of thousands of humans will surely die when they don't need to, will surely have horrible degenerative diseases that could be treated. Don't you take moral responsibility for them?"[60] Weissman argues for the value of embryonic stem cell research, but not all future therapies depend on ES cells. Adult stem cells, which raise no moral issues, hold great promise too.

## Tissue Engineering

In the future, scientists can even imagine growing whole organs for transplants from human stem cell lines. People who have had amputations or diseased kidneys or damaged livers might be cured with whole body parts grown in laboratories. This is called tissue engineering. In 1999, Dr. Anthony Atala used tissue engineering and adult stem cells to grow new bladders for six beagle dogs. Atala took bladder cells from the dogs and grew them in a special, biodegradable plastic mold that was shaped like a bladder. The cells grew

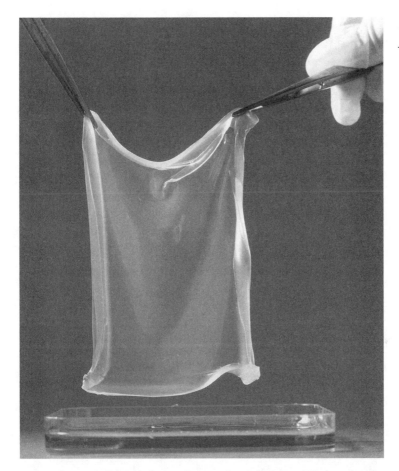

*A technician uses forceps to display a strip of skin grown with skin stem cells in a laboratory.*

into the mold and took on its shape. Then Atala removed the dogs' real bladders and transplanted the laboratory ones into the dogs. Within a month, the molds had biodegraded, the new bladders started working, and all the dogs could urinate normally. Since that time, Atala has grown a mini-kidney inside a cow and engineered blood vessels, muscles, and a womb for other animals. Using the knowledge he gained from these experiments, he even has grown urethras for humans. The urethra is the tube that comes from the bladder for voiding urine. People whose own urethras are damaged can function normally with Atala's lab inventions. Atala says, "The advantage of these engineered organs and tissues is that they are made from the patient's own cells so there is no risk of rejection."[61]

Atala's tissues are grown from adult stem cells. Unlike embryonic stem cells, these cells are difficult to grow in the lab and also hard to keep alive. Atala explains, "The big step forward was finding the right soup—the right combination of growth factors—that would make these cells grow."[62] Just like ES cells, adult stem cells need the right nutrition to live and proliferate. Atala's research has been so successful that he is almost ready to test muscles, bladders, blood vessels, and wombs in humans. People whose tissues were disabled from birth or whose organs have been damaged will benefit from tissue engineering.

Atala's experiments showed that cells grown together in the right environment signal each other and cooperate together. He says, "The cells know what to do. They have all the genetic information in place. You just have to give them the right conditions to do it in—the right temperature, the right nutrients. It's like baking a chocolate layer cake one layer at a time."[63] Growing blood vessel tissue or even a bladder is simpler than growing other organs. Blood vessels and bladders are thin and hollow, easier to fashion on a mold than more complex organs, but scientists are very encouraged by the early success of tissue engineering. Says one of Atala's colleagues, "It's an exciting area of science with endless possibilities. Imagine being able to create replacement organs from a patient's own cells."[64]

## Endogenous Cell Activation

Scientists are excited, too, about the future possibilities of endogenous cell activation—activation within the patient's own body, using its own stem cells. With this technique, the body's own inactive stem cells could be used to heal damage and disease. If researchers could learn enough from the stem cells they grow in laboratories about how stem cells are chemically coded, they could persuade adult stem cells in the body to turn on, start to grow, and repair

# Cloning

Scientists do not believe that true cloning, usually called reproductive cloning, is safe to try with people. Too many cloning attempts with animals have produced birth defects, genetic mistakes, and death. Cloning, however, has been successful with some animals and has the potential to save endangered animal species. In 2003, scientists at a company called Advanced Cell Technology (ACT) acquired frozen skin cells from an endangered banteng that had died at the San Diego Zoo. A banteng is a kind of wild ox that lives in the forests of southeast Asia. Few bantengs survive in the wild, and the male banteng that lived at the zoo had never mated and produced babies. It was the only male the zoo had. The ACT scientists unfroze the banteng skin cells and removed their nuclei. They put these nuclei into enucleated eggs from normal Angus cows. The eggs were then stimulated to begin dividing to the blastocyst stage. When the scientists had living preimplantation embryos, they sent them to an animal research center in Iowa where they were implanted into the wombs of ordinary cows. Two healthy banteng calves were born. The cloning procedure that ACT used is called cross-species cloning. This technique is exciting, not only to researchers at ACT, but also to zoo specialists and environmental scientists who worry about saving endangered animals. Without cross-species cloning, the San Diego Zoo would never have had another banteng.

*This cloned banteng is one of two that live at the San Diego Zoo.*

diseased organs. Adult stem cells in the human brain, for example, almost always stay quiet. That is why sick brains do not heal themselves as scraped skin does. Endogenous cell activation could turn on brain stem cells to make repairs and then turn them off again when the job was done. Dr. Mark F. Mehler at the Albert Einstein College of Medicine in New York thinks that this method will someday cure Alzheimer's disease.

Alzheimer's is a brain disease that robs people of memory and thinking skills. Eventually, the disease kills its victims, too. Although most Alzheimer's affects elderly people, some families carry an Alzheimer's gene that causes the disease to start when people are only in their thirties or forties. The gene is passed down through generations, with no way to know who will receive it and who will escape. These families, knowing they are doomed, search desperately for a cure. Today, their only hope is to avoid having children so that no more family members will be born with such a terrible death sentence. One woman whose family has early-onset Alzheimer's said, "I long for the day that my nieces and nephews, especially, will be released from the ghosts of their ancestors."[65]

Mehler and other scientists want to help people with Alzheimer's. The scientists are frustrated to know that adult stem cells sit in damaged brains, turned off, when they could be activated to heal the disease. Mehler has tried for years to find the chemical switches that tell brain stem cells to turn on and start to grow. "We know, though, that the signals will be there," he says, "not just for expansion and maturation of these stem cells, but their integration into neural networks, which is *really* important."[66] Just as Atala makes his nutritious soup, Mehler works in the lab to identify the chemical growth factors that activate adult stem cells in the brain.

Mehler's experimental growth factors may be ready to be infused into the brains of Alzheimer's patients within just a few years. He is not sure they will work, but he believes they will be safe and worth a try. He says,

> I think that the way it's going to happen is that people will put in one or another of their favorite growth factors and see what happens. . . . We're developing maps so that we'll know exactly which stem cells give rise to every cell sub-type in the brain. That means we'll be able to say the equivalent of, "OK, in subsector three of sub-zone 7, we need to activate that cell." And not only activate it, but activate it in a specific way.[67]

If Mehler and others succeed, they will have it in their power to cure Alzheimer's disease.

## An Endogenous Stem Cell Activation Success

When Dr. Mark Mehler predicted that scientists would soon try stem cell growth factors in Alzheimer's patients, he did not know how quickly he would be proved right. In April 2005, Dr. Mark Tuszynski at the University of California, San Diego, reported that he had tried a growth factor in eight people with Alzheimer's disease. Tuszynski and his team combined gene therapy with stem cell activation for their treatment. They took skin cells from their eight patients and changed the genes in the skin cells to include a growth factor. Then they surgically implanted these cells in the patients' brains.

In two cases, the surgery caused brain damage when the patients, numbed against pain but awake, moved during their operations. One of these people died. The other six people, however, were given general anesthesia to keep them still. They were operated on safely and their rate of brain cell death was slowed in comparison to other Alzheimer's sufferers. The patients did not get better, but they did not get worse either. This was a very successful outcome, because Alzheimer's always gets worse, and the death of brain cells has never before been slowed or stopped. The brain of the dead patient was analyzed and showed that new brain cells had grown because the brain's own stem cells were activated by the growth factors. The surviving patients all were at least 50 percent better at thinking and remembering than Alzheimer's patients who got no treatment.

The treatment was not a cure, but it encouraged doctors throughout the United States who search for an Alzheimer's therapy. Other researchers in other hospitals are trying the experiment to see if they get the same good results. If they do, the first treatment for Alzheimer's and other brain diseases may soon be here.

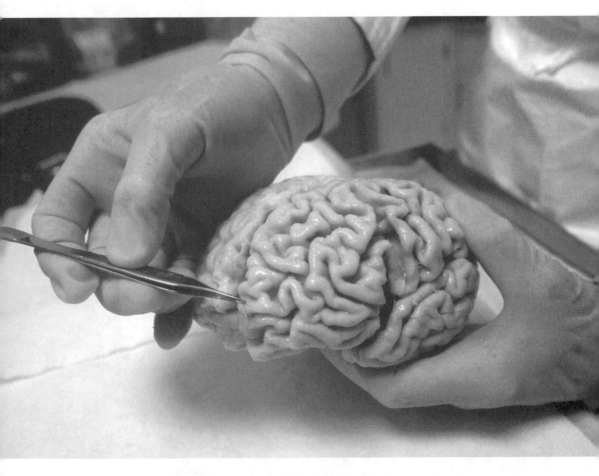

*A biologist at the University of Kentucky studies a diseased human brain as part of a research project on aging and Alzheimer's disease.*

## Unlimited Possibilities

Tremendous breakthroughs seem to lie in the future because of stem cell research. A few scientists have even experimented with changing multipotent adult stem cells into pluripotent ones, like embryonic stem cells. That would mean exposing adult stem cells to chemicals that make them younger, returning them to the embryonic state. No one is sure this is possible because so much remains unknown about the potential of stem cells. People with incurable diseases anxiously wait for the next research success and for human trials to begin. Because of the controversy over human ES cells, however, many people other than medical scientists control the pace of stem cell research.

# CHAPTER 7

# Regulation of Stem Cell Research

No one objects to adult stem cell research on moral grounds, but with embryonic stem cell research and therapeutic cloning, the situation is very different. The overriding issues are that an embryo is destroyed to retrieve its stem cells and that cloning violates the principle that only God should create human life. Since people disagree about whether such research is moral and defensible, both governments and scientific communities have regulated and controlled the processes. Decisions about what is right and what should be legal are deemed too complex and important to leave up to individual scientists.

## U.S. Government Policy

In the United States, legal boundaries of medical and scientific research traditionally have not been set by the federal government. Regulations have usually been left to the individual states. The federal government, however, does provide millions of dollars in funding for scientific research. The funding is given in the form of grants to different research laboratories. Most research is so expensive that it could not be done without federal grants. The government's National Institutes of Health (NIH) approves and conducts research and grants funds to laboratories that apply for money.

When President Bill Clinton first heard about the search for human stem cells in 1995, he appointed an ethics committee to help him decide whether the federal government should support it. Following the committee's recommendations, Clinton decided to allow some funding but with restrictions. The government would not pay for purchasing the embryos from in vitro clinics, would not fund the efforts to remove the stem cells from the blastocysts, and would not pay the cost of growing stem cell lines. After the stem cell lines were already grown, the government and NIH would fund research and experiments with them.

*In 2004 Californians voted overwhelmingly to allocate state money for stem cell research. Here, a researcher in a San Diego lab works with embryonic stem cells.*

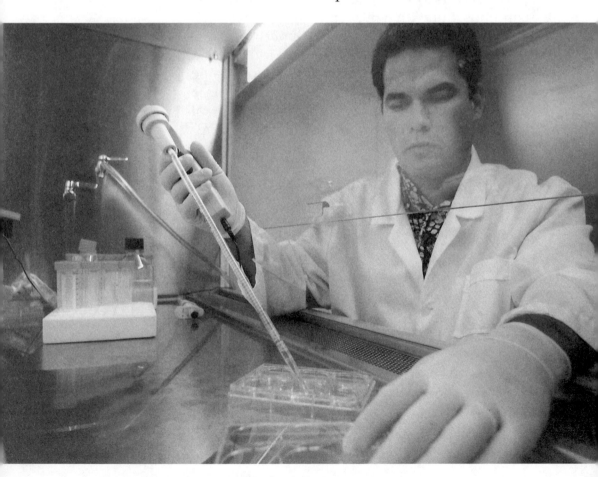

The decision satisfied no one. For some people, the Clinton decision was too restrictive and hurt the research. Others, however, wanted embryonic stem cell research to be outlawed altogether. In 1995, Congress voted to ban federal funding for any ES cell research. By 2000, the controversy had frightened many scientists away from embryonic stem cell research. Much of the government and the public was in an uproar, and no one could agree on what was right.

## Pressure for Change

The situation in 2001, when President George W. Bush took office, was bitter, and the country was divided. Bush was pressured to make a new decision. Bush appointed his own ethics council to help him decide. Most of these council members believed that human ES cell research and therapeutic cloning were morally repugnant because they involved the destruction of potential human life. The chairman, Dr. Leon Kass, once said about therapeutic cloning

> On the one hand, this research offers the prospect—though speculative at the moment—of gaining valuable knowledge and treatments for many diseases. On the other, it requires the exploitation and destruction of nascent life, and risks coarsening our moral sensibilities. Although individual council members weigh these concerns differently, we all agree that each side in this debate is defending something vital to us all: the goodness of knowledge and healing, the goodness of human life at all its stages. And each side must face up to the moral burdens of approving or disapproving of this research: namely, that some who might be healed in the future might not be, or that we will become a society that creates and uses some lives in the service of others.[68]

At the same time, others begged the president to allow funding for stem cell research. The National Research Council and Institute of Medicine concluded,

> Studies with *human* stem cells are essential to make progress in the development of treatments for *human* disease, and

this research should continue. Furthermore, stem cell research is just in its infancy and needs investment now, on both embryonic and adult stem cells. The work must be publicly funded, with open peer review and debate about the science and its potential clinical applications.[69]

## The Bush Policy

In the face of these contradictory opinions, Bush had to make a decision about government policy. On August 9, 2001, he gave a speech to the nation in which he described his decision and the reasons for it. He said, "As I thought about this issue, I kept returning to two fundamental questions. First, are these frozen embryos human life and therefore something precious to be protected? And second, if they're going to be destroyed anyway, shouldn't they be used for a greater good, for research that has the potential to save and improve other lives?" He admitted that he got different answers to these questions from the scientists, scholars, ethicists, citizens, and religious leaders that he consulted. He added, "Embryonic stem cell research offers both great promise and great peril, so I have decided we must proceed with great care."[70]

Bush decided that the federal government would fund embryonic stem cell research, but only if the experiments were done using the stem cell lines that had already been grown in laboratories. No new embryonic stem cell lines could be grown from embryos and funded with federal grants. Some people thought that Bush's decision was a thoughtful compromise, but many people were angry that the president had restricted funding so severely. Others were upset that Bush would grant any federal money to ES cell research and wanted it outlawed altogether. Nevertheless, the decision stood and is followed by NIH today.

NIH is the government institute that approves public funding for stem cell research according to the president's regulations. It follows three main rules in approving ES cell experiments. First, the only ES cells that can be used are those that were removed from a blastocyst before the date of the president's speech—9:00 P.M. on August 9, 2001. Any stem cell line started from a blastocyst after that date cannot be funded. The stem cells also must have been derived from an embryo from an in vitro fertilization clinic. Finally, the couple that donated the embryo must have done so without any financial reward. These rules ensure that the government does not fund the destruction of any embryos for research and that the ES cells that are used were acquired ethically.

## Citizens Lobby for ES Cells

Researchers in the United States have cooperated with NIH regulations since 2001, but few people are happy with the decision. Those who disapprove of

*President Bush authorized federal funds for stem cell research only on stem cell lines in existence prior to August 9, 2001.*

# When Does Life Begin?

For centuries, governments, citizens, and religious philosophers have argued about when human life actually begins. Thousands of years ago, babies were often not considered truly human until they had been born and named. Later, during the Middle Ages, many people identified the "quickening" as the point when a human existed. Quickening is the time when a woman first feels the movement of the fetus, usually when it is about four or five months old. In 1869, the Catholic Church chose the point of fertilization as the beginning of life. This is still the view of the Catholic Church and of several other Christian denominations. Other faiths had different standards. Both the Muslim and Jewish religions, for example, traditionally set the time that life begins at forty days after fertilization. An often quoted piece of Jewish law, for instance, says that until the fortieth day, embryos are "as if they were simply water." Today, many scientists choose the primitive streak as the stage that defines life's beginning. Others argue for the time when the embryo reaches the uterus, at day seven. Still others choose day twenty-two, when the heart begins to beat. So far, neither science nor religion has provided a certain answer that everyone can accept.

*Five days after fertilization, this human embryo is at the blastocyst stage of development.*

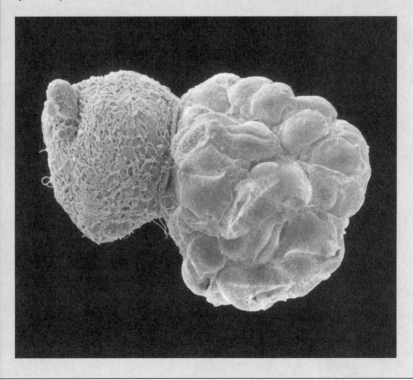

destroying embryos do not want to fund any stem cell lines. Supporters of ES cell research say that the approved stem cell lines are too few.

Several interest groups and scientific organizations lobbied Congress and the president to loosen the rules and allow research to move forward. Christopher Reeve, for example, testified before Congress in 2002, "While we prolong the stem cell debate, millions continue to suffer. It is time to harness the power of government and go forward."[71] The Michael J. Fox Foundation not only lobbied powerfully for stem cell research, but also began awarding its own grants to stem cell researchers in the hope that medical discoveries would not be delayed or stalled by federal refusal to allow new stem cell lines to be grown. The president of the foundation, Deborah W. Brooks, says, "Focused work in this area is an essential step for stem cell research in Parkinson's disease. We've made cell transplantation a top priority because we view it as a high-potential avenue of Parkinson's disease research that is currently underfunded by the federal government."[72]

## A Former First Lady Speaks Out

Nancy Reagan made pleas for federal funding for stem cell research, too, both in public and to President Bush personally. Her husband, former president Ronald Reagan, suffered from Alzheimer's disease, and she had seen firsthand how terrible it was and how much a cure was needed. Ronald Reagan no longer was able to recognize her and was dying. In a speech in 2004, Nancy Reagan said, "Ronnie's long journey has finally taken him to a distant place where I can no longer reach him. Because of this, I am determined to do whatever I can to save other families from this pain."[73] Her husband's suffering made her a strong supporter of stem cell research. She added, "Science has presented us with a hope called stem cell research, which may provide our scientists with

*Former first lady Nancy Reagan, whose husband suffered from Alzheimer's disease, is a vocal supporter of stem cell research.*

many answers that for so long have been beyond our grasp. I just don't see how we can turn our backs on this. We have lost so much time already. I just really can't bear to lose any more."[74]

## Some Are Persuaded, Some Seek Alternatives

Many people remained morally against human stem cell research, but the proponents' arguments did help to persuade others. Senator Orrin Hatch, for instance, was initially opposed to human ES cell research. He had originally said that he could not support anything that destroyed human life. In 2003, however, after hearing from many people with serious diseases, he began a philosophical journey that led him to change his mind. He became a supporter of funding the research. He explained, "I came to the conclusion that, yes, the fertilized egg is a living human cell, but it has absolutely zero chance of becoming a living human being unless it is implanted in a womb. It was difficult arriving at this point at which I could make a decision. But once I got there, it was easy."[75]

Others have not changed their positions. The Catholic Church, for example, remains opposed to embryonic cell research and has been active in supporting adult stem cell research as an alternative. The Vatican issued a statement in 2000 saying, "The possibility, now confirmed, of using adult stem cells to attain the same goals as would be sought with embryonic stem cells . . . indicates that adult stem cells represent a more reasonable and human method for making correct and sound progress in this new field of research and in the therapeutic applications which it promises."[76] Some scientists do believe that adult stem cells can be chemically persuaded to change from multipotent to pluripotent ES cells, but despite the church's statement, the process has not yet been proved.

## Contaminated Cells Complicate the Situation

Efforts to work with existing stem cell lines ran into trouble in 2005. Of the twenty-two human ES cell lines approved for experiments, scientists reported that all were contaminated and therefore useless for human experiments. The approved lines had been grown in nutritive baths that included mouse embryonic cells as growth starters. They could never be used for medical treatments because they would cause immune system attacks in human tissues. Scientists were frustrated and felt medical progress was being stalled by politics.

With this news, some members of Congress were ready to reconsider the federal limits on the funding of stem cell research. NIH officials publicly criticized the current restrictions on funding ES cell research, saying that they were slowing scientific progress. Because so few cell lines are available and because a 2004 poll reported that 74 percent of Americans support the research, Congress is considering a vote to loosen the regulations. President Bush, however, vows to veto any such change in the current policy.

## Outside Federal Guidelines

Public support for human stem cell research has encouraged some individual states to provide funding on their own. In 2004, Californians voted to support ES cell research with state funds. The state has decided to grant $300 million a year for ten years to California laboratories searching for medical treatments using ES cells. New Jersey also supports ES cell research. Several other states, including Massachusetts, Connecticut, New York, and Wisconsin, are considering such funding.

Meanwhile, as states argue about the ethics of stem cell research, private companies, universities, and nonprofit institutions fund ES cell research and develop their own ethics guidelines. The University of Wisconsin–Madison stem cell research program, for example, has an ethics committee that reviews all proposals and oversees human ES cell research. In 2001, this bioethics committee laid down rules for university research to ensure that such experiments were done with "an attitude of respect." The committee explained, "This respect suggests that research using human embryos should not be done without clear justification, and that human embryos should be used in the smallest numbers and at the earliest stages of development consistent with good science."[77] The committee recommended that embryos from in vitro clinics could be used only if the donors consented and understood what the research involved. Without ethics committee approval, experiments could not involve putting these embryos into a woman's womb or putting human ES

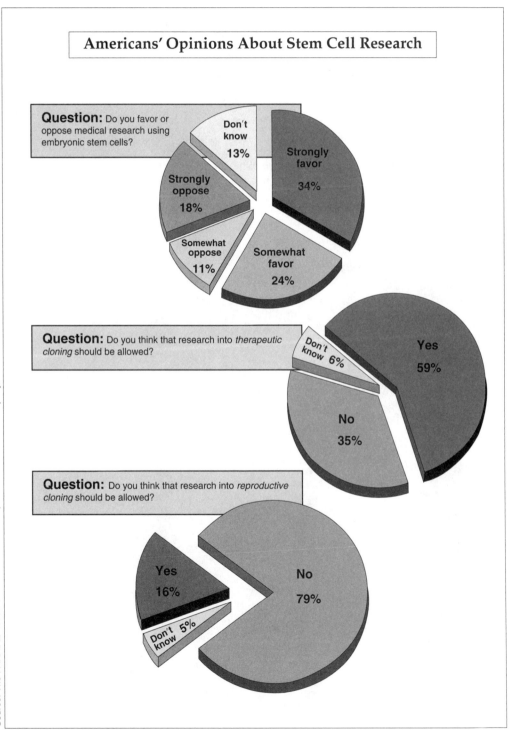

**Americans' Opinions About Stem Cell Research**

**Question:** Do you favor or oppose medical research using embryonic stem cells?

Don't know 13%

Strongly favor 34%

Strongly oppose 18%

Somewhat oppose 11%

Somewhat favor 24%

**Question:** Do you think that research into *therapeutic cloning* should be allowed?

Don't know 6%

Yes 59%

No 35%

**Question:** Do you think that research into *reproductive cloning* should be allowed?

Yes 16%

No 79%

Don't know 5%

Source: The PARADE/Research!America Health Poll, Charlton Research Company, 2005.

## Spain Goes for the Research

In 2005, the government of Spain decided to allow human embryonic stem cell research for the first time. The government chose four projects to approve and support with federal funding. The four projects are permitted to use only embryos from in vitro fertilization clinics and only those that have been frozen for at least five years. The parents also have to approve the donation of these unused embryos. The research experiments will involve a search for cures for diabetes, Parkinson's disease, and two tissue diseases. For five years, Spain's stem cell scientists had been fighting for permission to experiment with human ES cells. Spain is a Catholic country, but it has decided that the potential for good is too great to ignore. Spain's scientists are excited to at last be allowed to seek cures for diseases using human ES cells. Only three other countries in Europe currently allow human ES cell research: Great Britain, Sweden, and Belgium.

*A researcher works with embryonic stem cells at Spain's newly opened stem cell bank.*

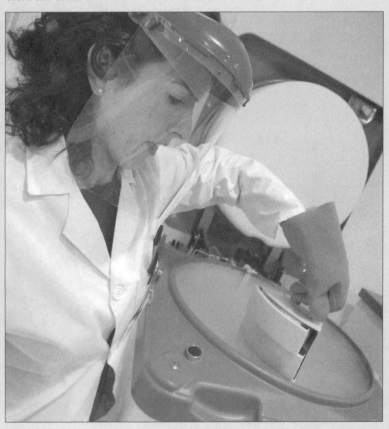

cells into animals. These regulations are similar to those followed at other institutions in the United States and around the world.

## Policy Choices Elsewhere

In many countries, especially Catholic countries, human embryonic stem cell research is outlawed altogether. Other countries, however, struggle with developing their own bioethics guidelines. In Great Britain, for example, human ES cell research is regulated by the Human Fertilization and Embryology Act. This act allows scientists to use discarded in vitro embryos to extract stem cells, grow stem lines, and attempt therapeutic cloning as long as the embryo is less than fourteen days old. This cutoff point was chosen because day fourteen of an embryo's growth marks the first possibility of cell differentiation into what is known as the "primitive streak." The primitive streak is a faint, dark line of cells, the earliest foundation of the body. It develops before any other body structure and may be the first point at which the cells can experience sensation. Many biologists believe that its appearance marks the beginning of life in any meaningful sense. Other countries, such as Singapore, Canada, and Sweden, also allow human ES cell research before day fourteen and define the appearance of the primitive streak as the true beginning of life.

## Going Forward

All over the world, people and governments are trying to strike a balance that values life, promotes scientific freedom, and supports the rights of all citizens. Scientists agree that the public must be informed and have accurate information if governments are to act wisely. In 2004, a coalition of more than 140 universities, scientific societies, and patient organizations wrote to President Bush asking him to reconsider federal policies. The letter said, in part, "Embryonic stem cells stand as a crucial link to the scientific puzzle that may

*As a result of stem cell research, diabetic Jamie Langbein (left) may see a cure for her disease within her lifetime.*

mitigate the pain and suffering of more than 100 million Americans and provide new therapies and other scientific opportunities for countless diseases such as diabetes, Alzheimer's, Parkinson's, ALS, heart disease, spinal cord injury, and cancer."[78] The Coalition for the Advancement of Medical Research believes that the more people are educated about the tremendous potential, the more they will support human stem cell research.

# Notes

## Introduction: The Promise of Stem Cell Research

1. Quoted in Connie Bruck, "On the Ballot: Hollywood Science," *New Yorker*, October 18, 2004. www.newyorker.com/printables/fact/041018fa_fact6.
2. Ann B. Parson, *The Proteus Effect*. Washington, DC: Joseph Henry, 2004, pp. 8–9.
3. Jane Maienschein, *Whose View of Life?* Cambridge, MA: Harvard University Press, 2003, p. 2.

## Chapter 1: The Discovery of Stem Cells

4. Quoted in Parson, *Proteus Effect*, p. 59–60.
5. Quoted in Joe Sornberger, "Canadians Till and McCulloch Proved Existence of Stem Cells," Stem Cell Network, vol. 3, no. 1, 2004, p. 3. www.stem cell network.ca/news/newsletters/news.summer 2004.en.pdf.
6. Quoted in Ruthann Richter, "Stem Cell Pursuits," *Stanford Medicine*, Winter 2002, http://ccis. stanford.edu/newsarticles/irv_stemcells_SM.htm.
7. Quoted in Joe Sornberger, "Weiss, Miller and van der Kooy Lead the Way in Neural Stem Cell Science," Stem Cell Network, vol. 3, no. 1, 2004, p. 10. www. stemcellnetwork.ca/news/newsletters/news. summer2004.en.pdf.
8. Quoted in Sornberger, "Weiss, Miller and van der Kooy Lead the Way in Neural Stem Cell Science," p. 11.

9. Quoted in Sornberger, "Weiss, Miller and van der Kooy Lead the Way in Neural Stem Cell Science," p. 11.
10. Quoted in Reuters, "Australian Scientists Grow Stem Cells from Nose," March 24, 2005. www.uspharmd. com/news/story/Australia_Scientists_Grow_Stem_ Cells_from_Nose_Reuters.html.
11. Quoted in Sornberger, "Weiss, Miller and van der Kooy Lead the Way in Neural Stem Cell Science," p. 11.

## Chapter 2: The Discovery of Embryonic Stem Cells

12. Quoted in Parson, *Proteus Effect*, p. 88.
13. Virginia Papaioannou, "An Interview with Martin Evans," Lasker Foundation, 2001. www.lasker foundation.org/awards/library/2001evans_int.shtml.
14. Quoted in Parson, *Proteus Effect*, p. 149.
15. Quoted in Parson, *Proteus Effect*, p. 174.
16. Quoted in JHMI Office of Communications and Public Affairs, "Hopkins Research Team Cultures Long-Awaited Human Embryonic Stem Cells," November 5, 1998. www.hopkinsmedicine.org/ press/1998/NOVEMBER/981105A.HTM.
17. PBS Online NewsHour, interview with Margaret Warner, July 10, 2001. www.pbs.org/newshour/ bb/health/july-dec01/stem_cells_7-10.html.
18. Pontifical Academy for Life, "On the Production and the Scientific and Therapeutic Use of Human Embryonic Stem Cells," Catholic Culture, August 25, 2000. www. catholicculture.org/docs/doc_view.cfm?recnum=3021.
19. Quoted in Parson, *Proteus Effect*, p. 173.
20. Quoted in Parson, *Proteus Effect*, p. 177.
21. Quoted in Richard M. Cohen, "Interview with Irving Weissman," Lasker Foundation, 2002. www.lasker foundation.org/news/weis/weissmant.html.

## Chapter 3: The In-Between Stem Cells

22. Testimony of Nathan Salley, July 17, 2001, United States House of Representatives, National Bioethics Advisory Commission. Reprinted in Michael Ruse

and Christopher A. Pynes, eds., *The Stem Cell Controversy*. Amherst, NY: Prometheus, 2003, p. 164.

23. Testimony of Nathan Salley in Ruse and Pynes, *Stem Cell Controversy*, p. 164.

24. Testimony of Nathan Salley in Ruse and Pynes, *Stem Cell Controversy*, p. 165.

25. Quoted in Cord Blood Registry, Real People, Real Stories, "Brandyn's Story." www.cordblood.com/cord_blood_banking_with_cbr/realpeople_realstories/index.asp.

26. Quoted in Alan Zarembo, "Selling Scientific Promise: A Desperate Injection of Stem Cells and Hope," *Los Angeles Times*, February 20, 2005. www.latimes.com/news/science/la-sci-stemcells20feb20,1,5329504,print.story?coll=...&ctrack=3&cset=true.

27. Quoted in Zarembo, "Selling Scientific Promise."

28. University of Minnesota Cancer Center, "Umbilical Cord Blood Transplantation," 2001. www.cancer.umn.edu/page/research/trsplant/cord3.html.

29. Quoted in University of Minnesota Cancer Center, "John E. Wagner, M.D.," 2003. www.cancer.umn.edu/page/research/trsplant/cord9.html.

## Chapter 4: Adult Stem Cell Therapies

30. Parson, *Proteus Effect*, pp. 48–49.

31. Quoted in St. Jude Children's Research Hospital, "Stem Cells: Reasons for the Research" (reprinted from *Promise* magazine, winter 2002), www.stjude.org/media/0,2561,453_2086_9410,00.html.

32. Quoted in St. Jude Children's Research Hospital, "St. Jude Researchers Prove Mesenchymal Cell Transplantation May Benefit Children with Osteogenesis Imperfecta," March 1, 2001. www.stjude.org/search/0,2616,582_3161_3304,00.html.

33. Quoted in St. Jude Children's Research Hospital, "Stem Cells: Reasons for the Research."

34. Quoted in St. Jude Children's Research Hospital, "Brave New Cells" (reprinted from *Promise* magazine, winter 2005). www.stjude.org/search/0,2616,582_3161_16749,00.html.

35. Quoted in St. Jude Children's Research Hospital, "Brave New Cells."

36. Quoted in St. Jude Children's Research Hospital, "Shandel Narcisse" (updated from *Promise* magazine, summer 2001). www.stjude.org/phecom/0,2777,632_4458_10402,00.html.

37. Quoted in St. Jude Children's Research Hospital, "Shandel Narcisse."

38. Quoted in St. Jude Children's Research Hospital, "Stem Cells: Reasons for the Research."

39. Quoted in St. Jude Children's Research Hospital, "Stem Cells: Reasons for the Research."

40. Quoted in St. Jude Children's Research Hospital, "Krista Mills" (reprinted from *Promise* magazine, spring 2003). www.stjude.org/search/0,2616,582_3161_9265,00.html.

41. Quoted in St. Jude Children's Research Hospital, "Krista Mills."

## Chapter 5: Using Embryonic Stem Cells

42. Gina Kolata, *Clone: The Road to Dolly and the Path Ahead.* New York: William Morrow, 1998, p. 122.

43. Quoted in Tom Clarke, "Mice Make Medical History," News @ Nature.Com, December 5, 2002. www.nature.com/news/2002/021202/pf/021202-10_pf.html.

44. Quoted in Nadia Halim, "Scientists Combine Therapeutic Cloning, Embryonic Stem Cells, and Gene Therapy to Correct a Genetic Defect in Mice," Whitehead Institute for Biomedical Research, March 7, 2002. www.wi.mit.edu/news/archives/2002/rj_0307.html.

45. Quoted in Joyce Gramza, "Human Cloning: The Science," ScienCentralNews, October 31, 2002. www.sciencentral.com/articles/view.php3?article_id=218391821&cat=3_2.

46. Quoted in CBS News.com, "Making Insulin Out of Stem Cells," November 19, 2002. www.cbsnews.com/stories/2002/11/19/health/main529925.shtml.

47. Catherine, Living with Diabetes, JDRF: Juvenile Diabetes Research Foundation in Australia, January 1, 2003. www.jdrf.org.au/living_w_diabetes/newsitem. asp?newsid=56.

48. Quoted in Kurt Ullman, "Stem Cell Transplants Help Repair Spinal Cord Injuries in Rats," WebMD Medical News, November 29, 1999. http://my.webmd.com/content/Article/20/1728_52645.htm.

49. Quoted in Washington University in St. Louis *Record*, "John McDonald Recognized for Spinal Cord Injury Research." http://record.wustl.edu/archive/1999/11-11-99/articles/mcdonald.html.

50. Quoted in *Johns Hopkins Magazine*, February 2001. www.jhu.edu/~jhumag/0201web/health.html.

51. Quoted in Embryonic Stem Cells: Research at the University of Wisconsin–Madison, "Stem Cell Findings Offer Promise for Heart Disease," June 26, 2003. www.news.wisc.edu/packages/stemcells/9064.html.

52. Quoted in Parson, *Proteus Effect*, p. 170.

53. Quoted in Paroma Basu, "Scientists Grow Critical Nerve Cells," Embryonic Stem Cells: Research at the University of Wisconsin–Madison, January 31, 2005. www.news.wisc.edu/packages/stemcells/10648.html.

54. Quoted in Basu, "Scientists Grow Critical Nerve Cells."

## Chapter 6: Hopeless No More?

55. Michael J. Fox, *Lucky Man*. New York: Hyperion, 2002, p. 214.

56. Susan Dentzer, interview with Dr. Ron McKay, PBS Online NewsHour, August 9, 2004. www.pbs.org/newshour/bb/health/july-dec04/mckay.html.

57. Christopher Reeve, "Why Do We Need Therapeutic Cloning?" Testimony by Christopher Reeve before the Senate Health, Education, Labor, and Pensions Committee, March 5, 2002. Printed in Christopher Reeve Paralysis Foundation. www.christopherreeve.org/hopenetwork/hopenetwork.cfm?ID=389&c=115&Type=s.

58. Quoted in Kolata, *Clone*, p. 229.

59. Gwen Ifill, interview with Leon Kass, "Human Cloning," PBS Online NewsHour, November 26, 2001. www.pbs.org/newshour/bb/health/july-dec01/cloning_11-26.html

60. Norman Swan, interview with Irving Weissman, "Stem Cell Research/Therapeutic Cloning," Health Report, Radio National, November 29, 2004. www.abc.net.au/rn/talks/8.30/helthrpt/stories/s1250698.htm.

61. Quoted in Wake Forest University Baptist Medical Center, "Internationally Recognized Tissue Engineering Program to Join Wake Forest University Baptist Medical Center," November 8, 2003. www1.wfubmc.edu/OTAM/OTAM+Quick+Info/News.htm.

62. Quoted in J. Travis, "Lab-Grown Bladders Prove a Success in Dogs," Science News Online, February 13, 1999. www.sciencenews.org/pages/sn_arc99/2_13_99/fob4.htm.

63. Quoted in Travis, "Lab-Grown Bladders Prove a Success in Dogs."

64. Wake Forest University Baptist Medical Center, "Internationally Recognized Tissue Engineering Program."

65. Quoted in Daniel A. Pollen, *Hannah's Heirs*. New York: Oxford University Press, 1993, p. 169.

66. Quoted in E.J. Mundell, "Brain's Own Stem Cells Might Fight Alzheimer's," Health Central, Get the Facts on Alzheimer's Disease, March 14, 2005. http://scc.healthcentral.com/bcp/main.asp?ap=408&brand=30&page=newsdetail&id=524474.

67. Quoted in Mundell, "Brain's Own Stem Cells Might Fight Alzheimer's."

## Chapter 7: Regulation of Stem Cell Research

68. Leon R. Kass, "Commentary: Stop All Cloning of Humans for Four Years." http://www.grg.org/LKass.htm.

69. Quoted in Maienschein, *Whose View of Life?* p. 288.

70. George W. Bush, Text of Bush Speech on Embryonic Stem Cell Research, Texans for Life Coalition. www.texlife.org/docs/bushspeech.html.

71. Christopher Reeve on Stem Cell Research, Your Congress.Com. www.yourcongress.com/ViewArticle. asp?article_id=225.

72. Quoted in Michael J. Fox Foundation for Parkinson's Research, "Michael J. Fox Foundation Boosts Stem Cell Research in Parkinson's and Awards Nearly $1 Million in Funding," January 31, 2005. www.michael jfox.org/news/article.php?id=145.

73. Quoted in CBS News.com, "Strong Plea from a Strong Lady," May 10, 2004. www.cbsnews.com/stories/ 2004/05/10/health/main616473.shtml.

74. Quoted in MSNBC News, "Nancy Reagan Urges Stem Cell Research," May 9, 2004. http://msnbc.msn. com/id/4937850/.

75. Quoted in *Clarkson Integrator*, "Senator Orrin Hatch Aborts Views to Support Stem Cell Research," February 17, 2003. www.clarksonintegrator.com/ news/2003/02/17/Features/Senator.Orrin.Hatch. Aborts.Views.To.Support.Stem.Cell.Research 372910.shtml.

76. Pontifical Academy for Life, "On the Production and the Scientific and Therapeutic Use of Human Embryonic Stem Cells."

77. Second Report of the Bioethics Advisory Committee on Human Embryonic Stem Cell Research at the University of Wisconsin–Madison. Embryonic Stem Cells, Research at the University of Wisconsin–Madison, November 7, 2001. www.news.wisc.edu/packages/ stemcells/bac_report2.html.

78. Coalition for the Advancement of Medical Research, June 23, 2004. www.camradvocacy.org/fastaction/ Change6-17-20042.pdf.

# GLOSSARY

**adult stem cell:** An unspecialized cell that can divide and differentiate to produce the cell types of the tissue in which it is found.

**antigen:** A protein that causes antibodies to form to fight infections in the body.

**blastocyst:** The embryo before implantation, consisting of about 30 to 150 cells in a ball.

**chromosome:** A structure in the nucleus of a cell that carries hereditary information in the genes and DNA.

**differentiate:** To become a specialized cell, such as a heart cell or a nerve cell.

**DNA:** The chemicals in the genes that carry the coding instructions for all body structures and functions. DNA is short for deoxyribonucleic acid.

**embryo:** The developing organism in the womb from the time of fertilization until the eighth week, for humans.

**embryonic stem cell (ES cell):** A primitive, undifferentiated cell in the blastocyst that is pluripotent and able to give rise to every type of cell in the body.

**endogenous cell activation:** Therapy that has its source in the patient's own stem cells, using growth factors to turn on those cells and regenerate healthy cells to replace diseased ones.

**enucleated:** With the nucleus removed.

**fertilization:** The uniting of the female egg and the male sperm.

**fetus:** In humans, the developing organism from eight weeks after fertilization until birth.

**gene:** A segment of DNA, on a specific point of a chromosome, that carries a specific unit of inheritance.

**graft-versus-host disease:** A condition in which transplanted infection-fighting cells from a donor recognize the cells in the patient, or host, as foreign and attack them as if the transplanted cells were fighting an infection.

**hematopoietic:** Blood-forming.

**immune system:** The system in the body that fights disease or invasion of foreign material. The immune system consists of many components including several kinds of white blood cells such as T cells.

**implantation:** The process in which the embryo embeds in the mother's womb. For mice, this happens on the fourth day after fertilization. For humans, it happens on the seventh or eighth day.

**inherited:** Caused by the transmission of genes passed on through families.

**in vitro fertilization:** Fertilization of an egg with sperm in a laboratory dish or other artificial environment.

**knockout mouse:** A mouse with one or more of its genes deleted or inactivated.

**mesenchymal:** Bone- and cartilage forming.

**multipotent:** Able to give rise to several types of mature cells, but not all. Adult stem cells are multipotent.

**myelin:** The insulating sheath that is wrapped around nerves and is necessary for their proper functioning.

**neuron:** A nerve cell.

**pluripotent:** Able to give rise to every kind of body cell but unable to generate the supporting fetal structures, such as the placenta. Embryonic stem cells are pluripotent.

**primitive streak:** The first band of cells to appear in the embryo. It establishes the head-to-tail structure of the embryo and will eventually differentiate into the three embryonic layers that give rise to the body.

**proliferation:** The continual multiplication of cells by the replication and division of stem cells into daughter cells.

**stem cell line:** Embryonic stem cells that have been grown in a petri dish where they proliferate without differentiating for a period of months or years.

**therapeutic cloning:** Cell nuclear transfer for treatment purposes. A body cell nucleus from a patient is transferred to an enucleated egg from which a genetically identical stem cell line can be grown and differentiated for use in medical therapy.

**totipotent:** Able to differentiate into all cell types. Only the zygote and its first few cell divisions are totipotent.

**transplantation:** A medical procedure in which a tissue or organ is removed and then replaced by a donor tissue or organ.

**unspecialized:** Having no ability to perform a specialized function, such as pumping blood or carrying oxygen. Unspecialized cells, however, can give rise to specialized cells. Stem cells are unspecialized cells.

**uterus:** The organ in the female body where a fertilized egg implants and develops; also called the womb.

**zygote:** The fertilized egg.

# FOR FURTHER READING

## Books

Geraldine Lux Flanagan, *Beginning Life*. New York: DK, 1996. This beautiful book follows the development of a new life from fertilized egg to newborn baby.

Susan Dudley Gold and Lillian McMahon, *Sickle Cell Disease* (Health Watch). Berkeley Heights, NJ: Enslow, 2001. This easy-to-read book tells the true story of Keone Penn, the first child to receive a stem cell transplant for sickle cell disease.

Robert Snedden, *DNA and Genetic Engineering* (Cells and Life series). Chicago: Heinemann-Raintree, 2003. Learn about gene therapy, cloning, transgenic animals, and the Human Genome Project.

Jenny Tesar, *Stem Cells* (Science on the Edge). San Diego: Blackbirch Press, 2003. Read about the discovery and uses of stem cells, as well as cloning and tissue repair.

Mary Dodson Wade, *ALS: Lou Gehrig's Disease*. Berkeley Heights, NJ: Enslow, 2001. Scientific explanations of ALS are combined with the stories of Lou Gehrig, Stephen Hawking, and others who have suffered this terrible disease.

Lisa Yount, *Cloning* (Contemporary Issues). San Diego: Greenhaven Press, 2000. A collection of articles on the science and ethics of cloning.

———, *Gene Therapy* (Great Medical Discoveries). San Diego: Lucent Books, 2002. The use of gene therapy is inextricably entwined with stem cell therapies and involves much of the same controversy. The reader can gain a full understanding of what genes are, how they work, and how scientists use genetic research to seek medical treatments.

## Web Sites

**Harvard University Gazette: Harvard Stem Cell Institute** (www.news.harvard.edu/gazette/2004/04.22/99-StemOver.html). Images, photographs, and videos explain the research at the Stem Cell Institute.

**How Stuff Works: What Are Stem Cells and What Are They Used For?** (http://science.howstuffworks.com/question621.htm). An easy-to-understand explanation of stem cells and several further links for information.

**JDRF Kids Online** (http://kids.jdrf.org). This is the official Juvenile Diabetes Research Foundation site for young people.

**Kids 4 Research: Diseases** (www.kids4research.org/diseases.html). At this site, the value of animals for medical research is described, along with the human diseases they have helped to cure. Information about knockout mice is here, too.

**Stem Cells: A Primer** (www.eamg-med.com/list/stem cells.shtml). A good, detailed discussion of stem cells that includes a glossary.

**The Visible Embryo** (www.visembryo.com). A remarkable spiral of images of the development of a human baby from zygote until birth.

# Works Consulted

## Books

Michael J. Fox, *Lucky Man*. New York: Hyperion, 2002. Fox describes his experience with Parkinson's disease and his journey to activism as a proponent of stem cell research.

Henry Gee, *Jacob's Ladder*. New York: W.W. Norton, 2004. This book details the history of the discovery of the human genome.

Ann A. Kiessling and Scott C. Anderson, *Human Embryonic Stem Cells: An Introduction to the Science and Therapeutic Potential*. Sudbury, MA: Jones and Bartlett, 2003. A detailed discussion of the science of embryonic stem cells, the research, the controversy, and the hope for the future.

Gina Kolata, *Clone: The Road to Dolly and the Path Ahead*. New York: William Morrow, 1998. The author tells the story of the science that led to the world's first cloned animal.

Jane Maienschein, *Whose View of Life?* Cambridge, MA: Harvard University Press, 2003. A thoughtful look at the controversy, politics, and science of cloning and stem cell research.

National Institutes of Health, *Stem Cells: Scientific Progress and Future Research Directions*. Honolulu, HI: University Press of the Pacific, 2005. A scholarly assessment of the history, the current state, and the future of stem cell research.

Ann B. Parson, *The Proteus Effect*. Washington, DC: Joseph Henry, 2004. The story of stem cell technologies, the discoverers, the researchers, the bioethicists, and the promise for the future.

Daniel A. Pollen, *Hannah's Heirs*. New York: Oxford University Press, 1993. A medical exploration of the generations of a family afflicted with early-onset Alzheimer's disease and their cooperation in the search for its genetic cause.

Christopher Reeve, *Nothing Is Impossible*. New York: Random House, 2002. A series of essays that Reeve penned, describing his life with a disability and his role as an advocate for spinal cord injury research.

Matt Ridley, *Genome*. New York: HarperCollins, 1999. The genetic history of humanity is explored, along with an explication of the Human Genome Project.

Michael Ruse and Christopher A. Pynes, eds., *The Stem Cell Controversy*. Amherst, New York: Prometheus, 2003. This book contains numerous thoughtful articles by different people covering a wide range of issues involved in embryonic stem cell research.

Nancy E. Snow, ed., *Stem Cell Research*. Notre Dame, IN: University of Notre Dame Press, 2003. A compilation exploring the science and ethics of stem cell research.

Michael D. West, *The Immortal Cell*. New York: Doubleday, 2003. A personal and scientific description of the quest to conquer aging and the mystery of life.

Lois Wingerson, *Unnatural Selection*. New York: Bantam, 1998. Genetic research and the ethical and legal dilemmas it engenders are explored and explained.

## Internet Sources

Paroma Basu, "Scientists Grow Critical Nerve Cells," Embryonic Stem Cells: Research at the University of Wisconsin–Madison, January 31, 2005. www.news. wisc.edu/pacjages/stemcells/10648.html.

Connie Bruck, "On the Ballot: Hollywood Science," *New*

*Yorker*, October 18, 2004. www.newyorker.com/printables/fact/041018fa_fact6.

George W. Bush, Text of Bush Speech on Embryonic Stem Cell Research, Texans for Life Coalition. www.texlife.org/docs/bushspeech.html.

Catherine, Living with Diabetes, JDRF: Juvenile Diabetes Research Foundation in Australia, January 1, 2003. www.jdrf.org.au/living_w_diabetes/newsitem.asp?newsid=56.

CBS News.com, "Making Insulin Out of Stem Cells," November 19, 2002. www.cbsnews.com/stories/2002/11/19/health/main529925.shtml.

———,"Strong Plea from a Strong Lady," May 10, 2004. www.cbsnews.com/stories/2004/05/l0/health/main616473.shtml.

Tom Clarke, "Mice Make Medical History," News @ Nature.Com, December 5, 2002. www.nature.com/news/2002/021202/pf/021202-10_pf.html.

*Clarkson Integrator,* "Senator Orrin Hatch Aborts Views to Support Stem Cell Research," February 17, 2003. www.clarksonintegrator.com/news/2003/02/17/Features/Senator.Orrin.Hatch.Aborts.Views.To.Support.Stem.Cell.Research-372910.shtml.

Coalition for the Advancement of Medical Research, June 23, 2004. www.camradvocacy.org/fastaction/Change6-17-20042.pdf.

Richard M. Cohen, "Interview with Irving Weissman," Lasker Foundation, 2002. www.laskerfoundation.org/news/weis/weissmant.html.

Susan Dentzer, interview with Dr. Ron McKay, PBS Online NewsHour, August 9, 2004. www.pbs.org/newshour/bb/health/july-dec04/mckay.html.

Joyce Gramza, "Human Cloning: The Science," ScienCentralNews, October 31, 2002. www.sciencentral.com/articles/view.php3?article_id=218391821&cat =3_2.

Nadia Halim, "Scientists Combine Therapeutic Cloning, Embryonic Stem Cells, and Gene Therapy to Correct a Genetic Defect in Mice," Whitehead Institute for Biomedical Research, March 7, 2002. www.wi.mit. edu/news/archives/2002/rj_0307.html.

Gwen Ifill, interview with Leon R. Kass, "Human Cloning," PBS Online NewsHour, November 26, 2001, www.pbs.org/newshour/bb/health/july–dec01/ cloning_11-26.html

*Johns Hopkins Magazine*, February 2001. www.jhu.edu/ ~jhumag/0201web/health.html.

JHMI Office of Communications and Public Affairs. "Hopkins Research Team Cultures Long-Awaited Human Embryonic Stem Cells," November 5, 1998. www.hopkinsmedicine.org/press/1998/NOVEM BER/981105A.htm.

Leon R. Kass, "Commentary: Stop All Cloning of Humans for Four Years." www.grg.org/LKass.htm.

Steve McVicker, "Bursting the Bubble," *Houston Press*, April 10, 1997. www.houstonpress.com./issues/1997-04-10/news/feature_print.html.

MSNBC News, "Nancy Reagan Urges Stem Cell Research," May 9, 2004. http://msnbc.msn.com/id/4937850/.

E.J. Mundell, "Brain's Own Stem Cells Might Fight Alzheimer's," Health Central, Get the Facts on Alzheimer's Disease, March 14, 2005. http://scc. healthcentral.com/bcp/main.asp?ap=408&brand=30 &page=newsdetail&id=524474.

Virginia Papaioannou, "An Interview with Martin Evans," Lasker Foundation, 2001. www.laskerfoun dation.org/awards/library/2001evans_int.shtml.

Pontifical Academy for Life, "On the Production and the Scientific and Therapeutic Use of Human Embryonic Stem Cells," Catholic Culture, August 25, 2000. www.catholicculture.org/docs/doc_view.cfm? recnum=3021.

Christopher Reeve on Stem Cell Research, Your Congress.Com. www.yourcongress.com/ViewArticle. asp?article_id=225.

Reuters, "Australian Scientists Grow Stem Cells from Nose," March 24, 2005. www.uspharmd.com/news/story/Australia_Scientists_Grow_Stem_Cells_from_Nose_Reuters.html.

Ruthann Richter, "Stem Cell Pursuits," *Stanford Medicine*, Winter 2002. http://ccis.stanford.edu/newsarticles/irv_stemcells_SM.htm.

Linda Sage, "Scientists Obtain Cells That Repair the Spinal Cord," Washington University in St. Louis School of Medicine, May 23, 2000. http://biology.about.com/gi/dynamic/offsite.htm?site=http://medicine.wustl.edu/%7Ewumpa/news/2000/mcdonaldpnas.html.

Joe Sornberger, "Canadians Till and McCulloch Proved Existence of Stem Cells," Stem Cell Network News Magazine, vol. 3, no. 1, 2004, www.stemcellnetwork.ca/news/newsletters/news.summer.2004.en.pdf.

———, "Weiss, Miller, and van der Kooy Lead the Way in Neural Stem Cell Science," Stem Cell Network, vol. 3, no. 1, 2004, p. 10. www.stemcellnetwork.ca/news/newsletters/news.summer.2004.en.pdf.

Norman Swan, interview with Irving Weissman, "Stem Cell Research/Therapeutic Cloning," Health Report, Radio National. November 29, 2004. www.abc.net.au/rn/talks/8.30/helthrpt/stories/s1250698.htm.

J. Travis, "Lab-Grown Bladders Prove a Success in Dogs," Science News Online, February 13, 1999. www.sciencenews.org/pages/sn_arc99/2_13_99/fob4.htm.

Kurt Ullman, "Stem Cell Transplants Help Repair Spinal Cord Injuries in Rats," WebMD Medical News, November 29, 1999. http://my.webmd.com/content/Article/20/1728_52645.htm.

Wake Forest University Baptist Medical Center, "Internationally Recognized Tissue Engineering Program to Join Wake Forest University Baptist Medical Center," November 8, 2003. www1.wfubmc.edu/OTAM/OTAM+Quick+Info/News.htm.

Margaret Warner, "Interview with John Gearhart," *PBS Online Newshour*, July 10, 2001. www.pbs.org/newshour/bb/health/july-dec01/stem_cells_7-10.html.

Washington University in St. Louis *Record*, "John McDonald Recognized for Spinal Cord Injury Research." http://wustl.edu/archive/1999/11-11-99/articles/mcdonald.html.

Alan Zarembo, "Selling Scientific Promise: A Desperate Injection of Stem Cells and Hope," *Los Angeles Times*, February 20, 2005. www.latimes.com/news/science/la-sci-stemcells20feb20,1,5329504,print.story?coll=...&ctrack=3&cset=true.

## Web Sites

**Advanced Cell Technology** (www.advancedcell.com/default.htm). ACT explains its mission, its research directions, and its latest advances.

**AlzheimersIssues.Com** (a member of the HealthScout Network) (www.alzheimersissues.com/). This very large site describes the symptoms, causes, and treatments of Alzheimer's. The future promise of stem cell research is well covered, too.

**Cord Blood Registry** (www.cordblood.com/index.asp). This private cord blood bank provides many stories about the value of saving cord blood.

**Christopher Reeve Paralysis Foundation** (www.christopherreeve.org/index.cfm). The foundation that Christopher Reeve established offers help to people with spinal cord injury and their families and friends. Here, everyone can learn about coping with spinal cord injury, current therapy options, and new research.

**Embryonic Stem Cells: Research at the University of Wisconsin–Madison** (www.news.wisc.edu/packages/stemcells). The University of Wisconsin–Madison has been in the forefront of ES cell research since James Thomson discovered human ES cells in 1998. Current research as well as general educational information is available at this site.

**The Jackson Laboratory** (www.jax.org/index.html). The nonprofit Jackson Laboratory is a leader in genetic research and the world's largest supplier of knockout mice.

**Michael J. Fox Foundation for Parkinson's Research** (www.michaeljfox.org/). The foundation is dedicated to funding research for Parkinson's disease in the hope of a cure. News and patient and family support are available, too.

**National Parkinson Foundation** (www.parkinson.org/site/pp.asp?c=9dJFJLPwB&b=71117). The official site of the National Parkinson Foundation offers information, help, and hope to people with Parkinson's disease.

**Stem Cell Information: The Official National Institutes of Health Resource for Stem Cell Research** (http://stem cells.nih.gov/index.asp). NIH provides extensive, detailed stem cell information to promote public awareness and education.

**Stem Cell Institute: University of Minnesota** (www.stem cell.umn.edu/). The university has a large research program dedicated to stem cell experimentation and is one of the nation's leaders in stem cell biology.

**St. Jude Children's Research Hospital** (www.stjude. org/). St. Jude's Web site describes the hospital's extensive medical efforts to treat and cure children and young people with life-threatening diseases.

**University of Minnesota Cancer Center: The Umbilical Cord Blood Transplant Progam** (www.cancer.umn.edu/page/research/trsplant/cord1.html). The Umbilical Cord Blood Transplant Program is explained for the benefit of patients, families, and the general public.

# INDEX

# PICTURE CREDITS

# About the Author

Toney Allman holds degrees from Ohio State University and University of Hawaii. She currently lives in Virginia, where she writes nonfiction books for students.